GROWING PEOPLE

.

GROWING PEOPLE

THE ENDURING LEGACY
OF JOHN DEWEY

NATALIA ROGACH ALEXANDER

Columbia University Press   *New York*

Columbia University Press
Publishers Since 1893
New York   Chichester, West Sussex

Copyright © 2025 Columbia University Press

Library of Congress Cataloging-in-Publication Data
Names: Alexander, Natalia Rogach author
Title: Growing people : the enduring legacy of John
Dewey / Natalia Rogach Alexander.
Description: New York : Columbia University Press, [2025] |
Includes bibliographical references and index.
Identifiers: LCCN 2025026260 (print) | LCCN 2025026261 (ebook) |
ISBN 9780231221894 hardback | ISBN 9780231221900 trade paperback |
ISBN 9780231563963 ebook
Subjects: LCSH: Dewey, John, 1859–1952 | Education—Philosophy |
Education—Social aspects | Democracy and education
Classification: LCC LB875.D5 A44 2025 (print) | LCC LB875.D5 (ebook)
LC record available at https://lccn.loc.gov/2025026260

Cover design: Julia Kushnirsky
Cover photograph: Natalia Rogach Alexander

GPSR Authorized Representative: Easy Access System Europe, Mustamäe
tee 50, 10621 Tallinn, Estonia, gpsr.requests@easproject.com

For James, soulmate and muse

CONTENTS

ACKNOWLEDGMENTS

I will always be grateful for the inspiring, dedicated, and supportive mentorship of my friend Philip Kitcher. Many of the ideas in this book were born in our engrossing conversations and in a period of immense intellectual growth and flourishing.

This book has been immeasurably enriched by conversations with Stuart Firestein, Robert Gooding-Williams, Axel Honneth, and Michele Moody-Adams. I thank them for their incisive comments and for many inspiring discussions about the issues I consider here. Many of the ideas in this project were developed in our dialogue, from which I learned a lot. I'm particularly grateful to Michele Moody-Adams for her work on democracy, which inspired me to develop many ideas for this book. I'm very lucky to have benefited from her intellectual companionship and inspiring example.

I'd like to thank Achille Varzi, whose joyful and imaginative approach to teaching showed me what education at its best looks like.

I'm deeply grateful to Wendy Lochner for her support and faith in this project.

Two anonymous reviewers contributed helpful comments, for which I thank them.

One of my earliest debts of gratitude goes to Steven Smith, who first ignited my interest in education as a fundamental philosophical issue. He has a way of asking questions one never forgets.

I thank my parents, family, and friends for their unwavering love and support.

Gratitude is too shallow a word to describe all I owe to James. It was his idea that I write this book. James stood steadfastly by my side through the inevitable ups and downs of the project. It is to him that I dedicate this book.

GROWING PEOPLE

INTRODUCTION

What is philosophy of education? The answer might seem obvious. When Plato deplores the influence of Homer on children's moral development, when Jean-Jacques Rousseau envisions getting Emile lost in a forest so that he may learn to draw his own maps, when John Dewey criticizes excessively bookish curricula that make learning "a mind-crushing load" (1916, MW 9:159)—they are all doing philosophy of education; criticizing existing practices of schooling and imagining new ones. The answer may seem so blatantly clear as to require no further elaboration.[1]

But if we look more carefully, we will see a richer picture. The philosophers I just cited embed their critiques of schooling in larger accounts of human development and flourishing. Plato doesn't just focus narrowly on arguing against exposing young children to stories of rage and sexual jealousy—he places that argument in a broader inquiry into the influence of mimesis on moral development. That account is, in turn, inseparable from his critique of how democratic politics might shape us. Plato is no less a philosopher of education when he questions democracy's effect on the soul as when he argues that the rulers of the ideal city should spend decades studying mathematics.[2]

When he laments the use of swaddling clothes in *Emile*, Rousseau might seem to sink decidedly below the level of serious philosophy.[3] But it is here that he makes some of his most incisive critiques of how modern bourgeois civilization "deforms" human beings. Examining nursery practices is part of a broader study of the nature and origin of domination in human societies. How do human beings develop vanity and the desire to control others? Can tyranny be stopped in the cradle? This connects to a still bigger question: Is it possible to create a social order based on freedom and equality?

Dewey is among the most famous philosophers of education of all time. But his best contributions to the field have never been fully appreciated. To be sure, plenty of books have been written about Dewey's "progressive" educational ideas: teachers should cater to each student's "uniqueness"; bookish learning should give way to socially engaged inquiry; active participation should replace passive absorption. A superficial reading suggests a picture of Dewey as a kindly educational reformer who wasn't a particularly deep philosopher. Active participation in the classroom may be good; it isn't philosophically interesting.

This superficial picture is wrong. Of course, Dewey's fame as an educational reformer is well founded. But we cannot understand his "progressive" views on schooling apart from his overarching inquiry into human development in all spheres of life. No study to date has fully captured Dewey's engagement in (and vision of) this ambitious project. No study has shown how this inquiry informed Dewey's work in other areas—political philosophy, aesthetics—connecting them in a coherent oeuvre that focuses on human growth. Yet this was his most important contribution to philosophy of education. Or so, at least, I will argue.

This book reveals a fresh portrait of Dewey as an educational theorist. It also offers a new perspective on a neglected field. Essential to the tradition I want to focus on is the broad enterprise of investigating and remaking the forces that shape who we become. Emphasizing this doesn't mean ignoring schooling. As Plato, Rousseau, Du Bois, and Dewey knew well, schooling shapes future generations. This is why they bothered to delve into the specifics of nursery practices, children's storytelling and vocational training. Still, what lent these more concrete discussions philosophical depth, richness, and critical force were the various fundamental perspectives on human development that informed them. As Dewey once put it, philosophy of education is about reconnecting schooling "to serious and thoughtful conceptions of life" (1916, MW 9:339).

Seen through this lens, underappreciated aspects of the philosophical tradition come to light, revealing the outlines of an "alternative canon" that focuses on human development. Central to this canon is the conversation that spans millennia between philosophers who took education seriously. Plato and Rousseau were Dewey's explicit interlocutors on education. But other authors are equally important to this canon. When, in "The Immortal Child," W. E. B. Du Bois connects reflections on the education of African Americans to a wider critique of racial oppression; when, in *A Room of One's Own*, Woolf criticizes women's unequal access to the conditions necessary for developing autonomy and creativity—they are making essential contributions to this canon.[4]

Like many other great philosophers, Dewey employed the past to serve his own philosophical agenda. One doesn't turn to Dewey for an unclouded view of the minutiae of Plato's arguments. Still, Dewey was a perceptive and original reader of the tradition. He was right on at least one point: the special importance of education to his interlocutors. Dewey was inspired by Plato and Rousseau because they, too, saw philosophy as a subject that seeks to investigate and facilitate human development and flourishing. He built on this insight to argue against the reigning view in philosophy that conceived of narrow, technical questions as paramount. Engaging with the past allowed him to create a platform from which to argue for a new way of doing philosophy—one that is relevant to solving the problems of the present.

Why am I focusing on Dewey? He is important as a thinker who sought to modernize the Ancient inquiry into human development and flourishing. Chapter 1 ("Philosophy and Education") shows how Dewey gave this inquiry a fresh start by drawing on historicism, evolutionary biology, and psychology (then a nascent field). Georg Hegel, Charles Darwin, and William James left an indelible mark on his thought. Taking them seriously meant that a simple return to the past was no longer possible. How should the ancient inquiry be continued today? How can this project be adapted to the challenges of modern industrial capitalist societies, to the problems of American democracy? Dewey tried to work out answers to these questions for the modern age.

With this general picture in place, chapters 2 ("Democracy and Education") and 3 ("Art and Education") reveal the centrality of education to Dewey's political philosophy and aesthetics. They show how Dewey's focus on human development helped him reorient debates in these fields. They also show what we can learn from Dewey as we face current challenges: the failures of contemporary democracies, widespread drudgery, estrangement among individuals and groups. Chapter 4, "Flourishing and

Education," revisits the idea of an "alternative canon" that focuses on human development.

Even the most wide-ranging and sympathetic reconstruction of Dewey's thought uncovers gaps in his immense oeuvre, which spans almost a hundred years and thirty-seven volumes. Dewey wasn't always right. But he is worth engaging with as the philosopher who provided the modern American answer to Plato's *Republic*.

The project of investigating and facilitating human growth in which Dewey so ardently believed remains unfinished.

It should continue.

1

PHILOSOPHY AND EDUCATION

§1.1. THEORIST OF EDUCATION

Those who think Dewey's philosophy of education is merely a collection of benign but banal ideas on "progressive" schooling should look at his works again. Taking the trouble to read Dewey carefully rewards us with a strikingly ambitious vision of the field. It will make us rethink our dismissive attitude. Not only did he put education at the center of philosophy, but he even said that it defines the discipline: "If we are willing to conceive education as the process of forming fundamental dispositions, intellectual and emotional, toward nature and fellow-men, philosophy may even be defined *as the general theory of education*" (1916, MW 9:338–39).

This is likely to make many readers cringe. Surely, reflections on the role of woodworking in schools don't exhaust the richness of the age-old discipline! Blinded by his own interests, Dewey reduced philosophy to kindergarten studies. Or so it might seem to the casual reader. Another way to react to this bizarre thesis is to reconsider what "theory of education" means. Carefully reconstructing Dewey's view reveals a vast, neglected

field of vital importance to modern societies. Kindergarten studies are part of it—but not the whole.

Philosophy as "theory of education"? Even charitable readers
will be puzzled by this. What about *Art as Experience*? *The Public and Its Problems*? *Reconstruction in Philosophy*? Dewey's own
works ranged widely over many topics, such as aesthetics, political theory, metaphilosophy. Was he inconsistent? We need a new
reading of Dewey, one that makes it clear why he made this
peculiar claim and whether he actually put it into practice in his
life's work.

This is a difficult task. Scattered throughout his works are
different theses about the relationship between philosophy and
education. The task is difficult because Dewey didn't tell us how
the pieces fit together. Sometimes, he says that education is sub-
stantively central to philosophy (philosophy is "theory of education"). At other times, he says it is methodologically central:
"Education is the laboratory in which philosophic distinctions
become concrete and are tested" (1916, MW 9:338–39). These
points are distinct. Perhaps they fit into a greater picture; Dewey
never tells us how. Then, of course, there is the problem of grasping how the view of philosophy as "theory of education" relates
to other definitions of philosophy he gave us. These, too, seem
distinct.[1]

The task is hard also because Dewey used the term "education" to mean different things. Sometimes it is understood
broadly as that "process of forming fundamental dispositions."
Clearly, he was also interested in schooling.[2] How do these fit
together? The picture becomes even more elaborate when we
appreciate that Dewey defined genuine education as "growth"—a
technical term that needs to be explained. In *Democracy and Education*, all these notions of education are invoked, sometimes
side by side: "the purpose of school education is to ensure

continuance of education by organizing the powers that insure growth" (1916, MW 9:56).

It isn't easy for Dewey's readers to see the true scope of his educational theory. The first step is to grasp the connection between education and the good life. His dialogue with Plato on this issue offers a particularly helpful entry point into Dewey's complex project.

§1.2. BACK TO PLATO

Readers familiar with Dewey's unequivocal rejection of Platonic epistemology and metaphysics might be surprised at the respect he had for Plato. A committed democrat, Dewey spent decades arguing against the rule of Platonic philosopher-kings.[3] But even when the two were most profoundly at odds, Dewey acknowledged the charm of Plato's "splendid and imperishable" vision (1888, EW 1:240–41). Plato's dialogues were Dewey's "favorite philosophic reading" (1930, LW 5:154). He found Plato's philosophy more "urbane" and "lucid" than that of the moderns (1925, LW 2:140). And Dewey wasn't merely a casual reader of Plato. *Democracy and Education* builds on his ideas: "Much which has been said so far is borrowed from what Plato first consciously taught the world" (1916, MW 9:94).

Even in his critique of modern philosophy, Dewey appealed to Plato: "Nothing could be more helpful to present philosophizing than a 'Back to Plato' movement" (1930, LW 5:155). What possible relevance could the ancient Athenian have in the modern context—as seen from the perspective of the consummate pragmatist? Dewey even credited Socrates and Plato with "bringing philosophy down from the heavens to earth" (1930, LW 5:289). This, too, might come as a surprise. In Book VI of the

Republic, Socrates envisions doing philosophy "without making use of anything visible at all, but only of forms themselves, moving on from forms to forms, and ending in forms."[4] Bringing philosophy down to earth? In Raphael's *School of Athens*, Plato is resolutely pointing upward.

The answer, of course, is that Dewey admired Plato not as a metaphysician but as a philosopher of education. When he credits the ancients with bringing philosophy "down to earth," he is thinking of their inquiry into "the possibilities of education in its largest sense" (1930, LW 5:289). In Plato's thought, philosophy and education went hand in hand. Education was conceived of as the means to the good life. Philosophy was the investigation of that life, "its constituents and . . . the conditions of its realization." The two were "organically connected" (1930, LW 5:292). Dewey wanted to restore that link. He appealed to Plato as his predecessor.

As Dewey imagines it, this was the moment when philosophy turned from the study of the "heavens" to human development. He even claims that all other philosophical questions arose out of the question: "Is education possible?" Dewey continues: "Because the query is so searching and so fundamental, it led into the raising of all the problems with which European philosophy since the time of the great Athenian has concerned itself" (1930, LW 5:290). Dewey's idiosyncratic vision of the origins of "all" philosophical problems may be historically inaccurate. Still, it clearly shows the importance he accorded to education. It was *the* lens through which he viewed the philosophical tradition. In Dewey's canon, philosophy originates in questions about whether—and how—we can be educated for the good life. In his canon, other philosophical inquiries are subsidiary. Properly pursued, they help facilitate human development.

"Is education possible?" The question might seem odd. Isn't the answer obvious? Various technical skills from carpentry to playing the piano are clearly teachable. To be sure, methods of instruction in many areas can still be improved. But it seems silly to ask whether education is possible at all. Dewey recognized this. What is at stake is neither "the possibility of training for skill in specialized callings" nor "the possibility of conveying successfully specific bodies of information." All this isn't "genuine education." What is at stake is "education as the deliberate initiation and cultivation of the good life" (1930, LW 5:290–91). Dewey isn't asking whether it is possible to teach carpentry or music. He's asking whether it is possible to educate human beings for a life of flourishing.

"Is education possible?" Now the answer appears less obvious. Can we really teach people to lead a flourishing life? If so, how? What character traits do we need to cultivate? What conditions have to be created for their cultivation? Who should be put in charge?

Once the *aim* of education is conceived in this broad way, the *scope* of education also widens. It includes "whatever contributes to the purposeful development of the good life" (1930, LW 5:290–91). This is "education in its largest sense" (1930, LW 5:289). To be sure, it includes schooling. But it doesn't end there. The educative influence of socioeconomic institutions needs to be considered, too. We might even need to take another look at a neglected area: the arts. This, of course, was just what Plato did.

Every reader of the *Republic* is familiar with Plato's hair-raising proposals for social reorganization: children are to be taken away from their parents at birth, all poets whose works are not approved by the state are to be banished.[5] What is less often appreciated is their proper context: an inquiry of unprecedented scope and depth into the forces that shaped the characters of his fellow Athenians. Grasping the importance of this inquiry doesn't require that we agree with Plato's proposals. Whatever we think of them, the *Republic* is valuable for the extraordinary project it contains: a critique of the educative influences of an entire culture and an attempt to imagine a radical alternative.[6]

In twentieth-century America, Dewey renewed the project. He appealed to Plato as a predecessor who challenged the prevalent customs: "In one thing at least our condition is similar to that of the Athenians. . . . We are no longer content to permit the work of teaching and discipline to take care of itself on the basis of precedent and unexamined models bequeathed from the past" (1930, LW 5:292–93). We moderns also face the task of taking a broad, critical perspective on all our educational practices, formal and informal. We face the challenge of redirecting them in the interest of enhancing flourishing. Instead of relying on "precedent and unexamined models bequeathed from the past," we should look at them afresh and try to take charge. This is what Plato did in his time. This is what we should do in ours.

From this standpoint, much modern theorizing about education appears too narrow. What are the forces that educate us? Who is—and who should be—in charge of the formation of our "fundamental dispositions, intellectual and emotional"? Such broad, seemingly intractable questions are largely neglected by contemporary philosophers.[7]

In "Philosophy and Education," Dewey imagined what Plato would have said about the current state of both enterprises. The answer wasn't flattering. "We are not . . . as far removed from the time of Socrates and Plato in insight as we are in years" (1930, LW 5:297). We moderns may have "more" education; but not of the right kind (1930, LW 5:292). Big questions about character formation and human flourishing remain unanswered. Worse still, they are often ignored and sidelined by both philosophy and education. Too specialized, too narrow to contemplate such questions, the two enterprises have parted ways. "Thought and attention have been diverted to details, and the sense of the encompassing whole has been blurred and often lost" (1930, LW 5:292). As a result, "education is now concerned with specialized and technical matters, not with the Good Life" (1930, LW 5:296). Philosophy has retreated to "a closeted seclusion" (1930, LW 5:297) to focus on arcane problems that have no relevance to human development. As Dewey saw it, Plato would have been thoroughly disappointed in us. Inspired by the Ancients, Dewey proposed a way forward. The key to it was taking education seriously—once again.

§1.3. THE MODERN PROJECT

Dewey was inspired by the ancients but not beholden to them. In one sense, his call for a " 'back to Plato' movement" was deceptive: he had no intention of turning back the clock. Much as he admired Plato, Dewey believed the ancient inquiry was due for a modern update. The complexities of modern societies generated problems unknown in Plato's time – for instance, the drudgery of factory work under industrial capitalism, which Dewey criticized in *Democracy and Education*. The extraordinary success of the sciences made the experimental method a new touchstone of inquiry. Inspired by it, Dewey formulated his own "empirical" method in philosophy. The Romantics illuminated the value of individual initiative and insight to social progress, which Dewey saw as a major advance over the ancient conception of the relationship of the individual and the community (1925, LW 1:164–69). Hegel, whose influence Dewey acknowledges in his intellectual autobiography (1930, LW 5:150–54), taught Dewey to see philosophy in historicist terms, as a child of its time. Darwinian evolutionary biology, coupled with William James's pioneering studies in psychology, offered a new, dynamic picture of life.[8] Literally "going back to Plato" was impossible. But his inquiry had to be continued. How?

To understand Dewey's answer, we need to grasp the contrast between his view and the position he attributed to Plato. Let's call the latter "Simple Platonism."[9] (Let's set aside the question of whether Dewey's understanding of Plato was accurate. This doesn't matter for my purposes. Even if he was wrong, it helps clarify Dewey's own project.)

Simple Platonism holds that the philosopher has some privileged access to the eternal, fixed pattern of the Good. It seeks to institute that pattern in the lives of individuals and communities. Simple Platonism values stability and distrusts change. Its goal is permanent harmony. To institute the ideal way of life once and for all, it calls for radical, wholesale social reorganization. This involves purifying all the current educative practices. Studying mathematics and music helps promote the perfect way of life; these subjects are prioritized. Telling Homer's stories to children induces dangerous passions that threaten the Ideal City; they are banned. Purifying education is a means of instituting a perfect, fixed way of life—forever.

Democracy and Education makes Dewey's disagreement with Simple Platonism clear. Having acknowledged his debt to Plato (1916, MW 9:94), he offers a critique:

> Although his educational philosophy was revolutionary, it was none the less *in bondage to static ideals*. He thought that change or alteration was evidence of lawless flux; that true reality was

unchangeable. Hence while he would radically change the existing state of society, *his aim was to construct a state in which change
would subsequently have no place. The final end of life is fixed*; given
a state framed with this end in view, not even minor details are
to be altered. . . . The breakdown of his philosophy is made appar-
ent in the fact that *he could not trust to gradual improvements in
education to bring about a better society which should then improve
education, and so on indefinitely.* Correct education could not come
into existence until an ideal state existed, and after that education would be devoted simply to its conservation. *For the existence
of this state he was obliged to trust to some happy accident* by which
philosophic wisdom should happen to coincide with possession
of ruling power in the state. (1916, MW 9:97, my emphases)

As Dewey saw it, Simple Platonism's hope that the philosopher
who knows the final end of existence might come to power by
"happy accident" is utopian. This passage hints at Dewey's
meliorist alternative. He didn't seek perfect education in order
to institute a static, ideal society. He wanted gradually to improve
education in order to improve society. Having made progress,
humanity would improve education further. "And so on indefinitely." Although we might formulate some local ideals ("ends-
in-view"), "the final end of life" isn't fixed—or known.

Lest you think that Dewey was utterly uncharitable to Simple Platonism, recall that he once called the Ideal City of the
Republic "a splendid and imperishable vision" (1888, EW 1:240–
41). Its charm is obvious. If it were the case that the philosopher
could have access to the eternal pattern of the Good; if that Good
were attainable once and for all in just the way the Simple Platonist envisages, the Ideal City would, of course, be ideal.

Clearly Dewey respected Plato's "revolutionary" educational
ideas. Clearly he was inspired by the ancient Athenian's project

of criticizing educational practices in the interest of improving society. But he was a meliorist. Dewey believed in enhancing human flourishing by constantly identifying and eradicating specific sources of confinement and suffering—without formulating a complete, fixed, and final account of what a perfectly flourishing life looks like.

Nor did he share the Simple Platonist's aversion to flux. Dewey celebrated it. As he saw it, Darwin's work had revolutionary implications for philosophy: "it introduced a new intellectual temper." This new philosophical disposition rejects "the superiority of the fixed and final" in favor of investigating and embracing change (1909, MW 4:3). It abandons the quest for perfection in favor of making incremental improvements in the here and now. Dewey anticipated that this shift in temper would have a profound effect on many fields—politics, morals, religion, and education.

Inspired by "the new temper," in *Democracy and Education* Dewey proposed a fresh perspective on the formation of our "fundamental dispositions." Education isn't about cultivating a fixed and perfect character with some complete and final account of human flourishing in mind. It is about facilitating "growth" (1916, MW 9:56). In the rest of this book, I shall say a lot more about the details of this view. For my present purposes, a brief overview will suffice to make the contrast with Simple Platonism clear. Growth is the constant, never-ending revision of our individual and collective habits in the interest of gradually enhancing human flourishing. In Dewey's scheme, education isn't a means to bring about a predefined, fixed, ideal form of communal and individual life. It is there to facilitate continual human development. Its aim is to create an evolving society—one that develops itself by constantly solving the new problems it faces in order to reduce human suffering and liberate human capacities.

The community it seeks develops in a direction set by its members, who have attained the capacity to take part in defining and seeking the good life together. On this view, flourishing isn't something we can attain once and for all. New problems keep emerging. Developing sensitivities disclose hitherto underappreciated sources of confinement and suffering. New powers create new needs. We never get to permanent, wholesale harmony. What we need is a continuous evolution of our individual and collective habits.[10]

In chapter 24 of *Democracy and Education*, Dewey offers us a novel picture of the philosophic disposition. It's oriented not towards a fixed state of harmony, but toward the constant growth of our individual and communal habits. The philosophic wholeness of being is reconceived here in a characteristically Deweyan way: it is "the carrying on of a former habit of action with the readaptation necessary to keep it alive and *growing*" (my emphasis). The philosophic attitude is one of "open-mindedness" and "sensitivity to new perceptions." It involves "an ability to go on learning" in light of new challenges, constantly revising existing habits (1916, MW 9:335–36).

Now we can offer a further gloss on Dewey's bizarre definition of philosophy as "theory of education" (1916, MW 9:338–39). He isn't saying that kindergarten studies exhaust the age-old discipline. Nor is he envisaging philosophy as formulating some wholesale and permanent vision of flourishing, to be instituted with the help of proper education. Philosophy should investigate and facilitate human development. As I shall argue later, schooling plays an important part in this bigger project. Earlier we saw that Dewey was inspired by Plato to think of education as the means to "a good life" (1930, LW 5:292). Now we have a more sophisticated grasp of Dewey's view: schooling (and other educative practices) are important instruments of human development in the interest of making gradual enhancements to human flourishing.

Recall the question Dewey thought gave rise to "all" the questions of philosophy. "Is education possible?" I have saved Dewey's most provocative gloss on it until now. "Is education really possible, means: Is it possible to apply intelligence intentionally and systematically to the regulation of life?" (1930, LW 5:290) This is perhaps the clearest formulation he ever gave of one of his philosophy's most fundamental questions. (This, as Dewey recognized, was also one of Plato's central concerns.) What is at stake is whether we can take charge of human development. Few questions are more momentous. Now we are far away from the view of philosophy of education as a superficial field of interest to schoolteachers alone.

§1.4. SCHOOLING REVISITED

You might think Dewey's favorite topic—schooling—has dropped out of the picture I have been painting. It hasn't. Once we have grasped Dewey's larger project, we can clearly see why schooling matters. He believed that "the more conscious and formal education" is "the most economical and efficient means of social advance and reorganization" (1920, MW 12:186). Schooling is an instrument of human development.

In *Democracy and Education*, Dewey contrasts education in static societies with his own democratic view. Static societies use schooling to maintain established customs (1916, MW 9:85). In such societies, education is merely "a sort of catching up of the child with the aptitudes and resources of the adult group" (1916, MW 9:85). Dewey wants to go further: "progressive communities . . . endeavor to shape the experiences of the young so that instead of reproducing current habits, better habits shall be formed, and thus the future adult society be an improvement on their own" (1916, MW 9:85). Here the linkage between schooling and human development is explicit. When Dewey talks about educating children, he is simultaneously discussing creating the society of the future: "education . . . represents not only *a development* of children and youth but also *of the future society* of which they will be constituents" (1916, MW 9:85, my emphasis). He isn't addressing teachers alone. He's talking to all those who care about realizing "the better hopes" (1916, MW 9:85) of humanity.

Of course, schooling alone won't magically make societies better. Dewey understood this. Individual human beings have to do the work. Properly educated, they can do it—in conversation with each other. What Dewey wanted wasn't just an educational program that would improve society once, "by some magic of its own."[11] He wanted schooling to prepare human beings to take charge of their personal and social growth. This view is central to *Democracy and Education*, in which Dewey envisaged a program of schooling that "forms character which . . . is interested in that continuous readjustment which is essential to growth," social and individual (1916, MW 9:370). And it is echoed in later works: "I do not believe that anyone can accurately predict what the future will bring forth or set up adequate ideals of future society. But in the degree in which education develops individuals into mastery of their own capacities, we must trust these individuals to meet issues as they arise, and *to remake the social conditions they face into something worthier of man and life*" (1930, LW 5:297, my emphasis).

This sheds new light on Dewey's famous "progressive" educational ideas. He didn't recommend creating cooperative classrooms simply because he was kindhearted. The methods he championed were the result of serious philosophical reflection on how we can create evolving societies, how we can educate individuals to engage in continual social reorganization. They are part of Dewey's answer to the "big" question I touched on earlier: "Is it possible to apply intelligence intentionally and systematically to the regulation of life?" (1930, LW 5:290).

At its best, schooling can prepare human beings for a life of "growth" (1916, MW 9:370). At its worst, it can confine and oppress them. Education isn't just a method for "social advance and reorganization" (1920, MW 12:186). It's also an instrument in the "art of social control" (1925, LW 1:104). The philosophers who took schooling seriously imagined how they could use it to create a better world. They also criticized the way it was used in their time to keep the world as it was. Central to the *Republic* is the debate on who should have the authority to educate the young. Plato recognized the power that goes along with having that authority. As Plato saw it, the educative practices of his time kept the prisoners in the cave. Perceiving the world through the prism of the Homeric narratives they had been taught at a young age, his fellow Athenians failed to understand the world and one another.[12] In *Emile*, Rousseau argued that the use of swaddling clothes creates little tyrants who perpetuate the inequalities and injustices of the modern bourgeois societies he held in such contempt.

This approach is particularly striking in W. E. B. Du Bois's writings. He often made schooling a focal point for his critique of racial oppression. Du Bois saw that the education African Americans received in his time perpetuated racial injustice. This is what is at stake in the biting, incisive commencement addresses he delivered throughout his career, collected in *The Education of Black People: Ten Critiques*. The theme is also present in *The Souls of Black Folk*, in which he writes, "we daily hear that an education that encourages aspiration, that sets the loftiest of ideals and seeks as an end culture and character rather than bread-winning, is the privilege of white men and the danger and delusion of black."[13] Du Bois saw educational reform as an important instrument in the project of overcoming racial oppression. *The Souls of Black Folk* eloquently captures Du Bois's vision of how this was to be achieved: "there must come a loftier respect for the sovereign human soul that seeks to know itself and the world about it; that seeks a freedom for expansion and self-development; that will love and hate and labor in its own way, untrammeled alike by old and new."[14] Dewey never gave anything like the deep analysis that Du Bois offered of the ways that racial oppression is maintained through education. Still, the two thinkers were allies in their critiques of how defective schooling "hems in" human beings. They were allies, too, in seeing schooling as a means to social progress.

Together with Du Bois's *Ten Critiques*, Dewey's examination of the then-prevalent methods of schooling in *Democracy and Education* was an important chapter in the history of American social criticism. He was worried that overly authoritarian teaching styles foster docility and obedience, creating citizens who are easy to manipulate and take advantage of (1916, MW 9:159–60). They stifle initiative and prevent communal growth. Such practices help buttress a social order that keeps a large mass of people in a state of servility. The rigid separation of vocational and liberal studies further exacerbates the problem (1916, MW 9:332).

Now we have a fresh perspective on Dewey's most famous book. *Democracy and Education* is commonly read as a handbook for "progressive" teachers. But it is much more than that. The book is part of a large, important philosophical project that focuses on human development. If schooling can facilitate "social advance and reorganization," no philosophy that seeks such reorganization is complete without discussing education in this narrow sense. Philosophers should take it seriously—just as did Plato, Rousseau, Dewey, and Du Bois.

§1.5. THE SUPREME TEST

"Philosophy is theory of education." It isn't hard to see how this applies to Dewey's works on schooling. What is less obvious is how his other works fit this bizarre definition. His thirty-seven-volume oeuvre covers many issues beyond schooling: the democratic ethos, the value of speculative philosophy, even the role of museums in capitalist America. A clue is given in *Reconstruction in Philosophy*, the manifesto of Dewey's pragmatism:

> *The test of all the institutions of adult life is their effect in furthering continued education.*
>
> Government, business, art, religion, all social institutions have a meaning, a purpose. That purpose is to set free and to develop the capacities of human individuals without respect to race, sex, class or economic status. And this is all one with saying that *the test of their value is the extent to which they educate every individual into the full stature of his possibility*. Democracy has many meanings, but if it has a moral meaning, it is found in resolving that *the supreme test of all political institutions and industrial arrangements* shall be the contribution they make to the all-round *growth* of every member of society. (1920, MW 12:186, my emphases)

All our practices and institutions should be reassessed in light of their educative effects.

"Growth" lies at the center of this critique. A few pages later, growth is defined as the "release of capacity from whatever hems it in" (1920, MW 12:198–99). What Dewey is suggesting is that we "test" the value of socioeconomic arrangements and other practices by asking whether they enable the release of human capacities. Here he moves beyond schooling to consider "education in its largest sense" (1930, LW 5:289). This aligns with the Plato-inspired program I outlined earlier.

Another point of Dewey's pragmatic manifesto comes to light in the passage just quoted. Motivating much of what he wrote was his profound faith in the importance of making "the good life" open to all human beings. Dewey took the flourishing of the "mass" seriously. Pursuing this commitment, his works seek to identify existing barriers to human flourishing on a broad scale. Some works take up the division between vocational and liberal pursuits, they lament the confinement of the "mass" to unfulfilling work (e.g. 1916, MW 9, and 1930, LW 5:41–123). Others critique the separation of fine arts from ordinary human lives; they seek to recover and extend sources of beauty in the everyday existence of "regular" human beings (1934, LW 10). Still other works argue for a democratic way of life that progressively overcomes confining prejudices (1922, MW 13:242–54; 1939, LW 14:91–97; 1939, LW 14:224–30; 1940, LW 14:258–61). Some pieces attack the assumption that mediocrity is the inevitable fate of the "mass" (1922, MW 13:289–94; 1922, MW 13:295–300). Even Dewey's most abstract work that offers a new theory of experience and inquiry—*Experience and Nature*—takes up this theme: "The more aware one is of the richness of meanings which experience possesses, the more will a generous and catholic thinker be conscious of the limits which prevent sharing in them; the more aware will he be of their accidental and arbitrary distribution" (1925, LW 1:308).

Did Dewey try to dilute the richness of human experience, bringing it to the lowest common denominator? This passage indicates he didn't. Uncharitable readers might take Dewey's interest in "ordinary" life as a sign that he failed to appreciate the more refined kinds of experience. His analysis of modern painting in *Art as Experience* shows the contrary. Dewey wasn't unsophisticated. He was a "generous" thinker in the sense defined above: he wanted "the best, the richest and fullest experience possible" for all (1925, LW 1:308). His commitment to making the good life open to all isn't tantamount to embracing and celebrating mediocrity, as critics might fear (1922, MW 13:289–300). It is a commitment to developing each individual's capacities and fostering uniqueness.

Reconstruction in Philosophy gives us another formulation of Dewey's program:

> Just what response does *this* social arrangement, political or economic, evoke, and *what effect does it have upon the disposition* of those who engage in it? Does it release capacity? If so, how widely? Among a few, with a corresponding depression in others, or in an extensive and equitable way? . . . Such questions as these . . . become the starting-points of inquiries about every institution of the community when it is recognized that individuality is not originally given but is created under the influences of associated life. . . . *What sort of individuals are created?* (1920, MW 12:193, my emphases)

The two formulations are in harmony, since the answer to the question "What sorts of individuals are created?" is determined, at least in part, by how their capacities are developed. Recall that Dewey's bizarre definition of philosophy as "theory of education" takes education to be "the formation of our fundamental dispositions." The passage I just quoted focuses on education in this sense. Philosophy of education isn't just about schooling; it's also about considering the effect of various social arrangements on our "dispositions." The key assumption of this project is also captured here: "individuality is not originally given but is created under the influences of associated life." The enterprise is guided by the idea that the way we live together is an important determinant of who we become. Hence the need to extend philosophy of education to consider the broader educative influences of "associated life."

Now we start to see the answer to the puzzle of how Dewey's works fit together. Schooling isn't the only site of education, broadly conceived as the formation of our "fundamental dispositions." Other practices and institutions are also crucial. Like Plato, Dewey understood this. Like Plato's, Dewey's philosophy of education was an even bigger project. "What sort of individuals are created?" He wanted us to ask this question "about *every* institution of the community" (1920, MW 12:193, my emphasis). In his oeuvre, education broadly conceived serves as the touchstone for philosophical inquiry in many fields—political philosophy, aesthetics, even metaphilosophy.

Philosophy of education is about theorizing how schools can help us build a better world. It's also about examining how various existing practices and institutions shape us. The two projects are related. In Dewey's works, diagnosing the failures of the current socioeconomic arrangements goes hand in hand with imagining how schooling could play a role in creating and sustaining better ones (that would, in turn, have better broad educative effects). Understood this way, philosophy of education involves sweeping social critique. This takes us even further from the shallow view that "theory of education" is a boring field.

§1.6. WAYS OF LIVING

By now, we're starting to get a sense of the richness and complexity of Dewey's theory of education. But the picture isn't complete yet. Further nuance is added once we grasp his view that philosophy itself should be criticized in light of how it shapes us.

Democracy and Education defines philosophy in terms of the "fundamental dispositions" to which it corresponds. As usual, Dewey appeals to the ancients: "almost all ancient schools of philosophy were also organized ways of living" (1916, MW 9:334).[15] A contrast with science helps him make his point clear. Science gives us facts about the world; philosophy seeks the right attitude toward the known. Philosophy shouldn't be defined exclusively with respect to its subject matter. It should be seen as a way of life. "Philosophy is thinking what the known demands of us—what responsive attitude it exacts" (1916, MW 9:336).

Philosophy can be a deeply personal way of life.[16] Dewey recognized this, as is clear in his discussion of "homespun philosophies": "Often these clashes between various interests can be settled by the individual for himself; the area of the struggle of aims is limited and a person works out his own rough accommodations. Such homespun philosophies are genuine and often adequate. But they do not result in systems of philosophy. These arise when the discrepant claims of different ideals of conduct *affect the community as a whole, and the need for readjustment is general*" (1916, MW 9:336, my emphasis). But philosophy as a personal way of life wasn't his main focus. He was interested in philosophy as a practice that influences human development on a broader scale, affecting "the community as a whole." *Reconstruction in Philosophy* suggests that we "study the history of philosophy not as an isolated thing but as a chapter in the development of civilization and culture." In line with this, Dewey's works seek to "connect the story of philosophy with a study of anthropology, primitive life, the history of religion, literature and social institutions" (1920, MW 12:93).

Recall the task laid out in Dewey's pragmatic manifesto: all our practices and institutions ought to be reassessed in light of how they shape us. Philosophy itself is covered by this program. Now we can see how his central "theoretical" works (*The Quest for Certainty*, *Experience and Nature*, *Reconstruction in Philosophy*) fit into the picture I have been painting.

In *Reconstruction in Philosophy*, the idea of the ready-made world is rejected because it results in "intellectual irresponsibility and neglect" (1920, MW 12:135). Hegel's theory gets criticized, too, for embracing an attitude of "acquiescence" (1920, MW 12:90). In *Experience and Nature*, idealistic philosophies are charged with encouraging "sentimental indulgence" and a "flight from the hardships of life" (1925, LW 1:325). "Spectator" theories of knowledge are rejected, too, because they foster "carelessness and routine, Olympian aloofness, secluded contemplation" (1925, LW 1:326). This is echoed in *The Quest for Certainty* (1929, LW 4).

In each instance, traditional philosophies are criticized based on the "fundamental dispositions" they create. In each instance, education broadly conceived serves as a touchstone for metaphilosophical critique. In *Experience and Nature* Dewey suggests that we think of traditional philosophies as having been "tried" and having failed (1925, LW 1:326). They failed, he thinks, because they fostered unhelpful, even confining, attitudes.

Dewey lays out his philosophical method in *Experience and Nature*:

What empirical method exacts of philosophy is two things: First, that refined methods and products be *traced back to their origin in primary experience*, in all its heterogeneity and fullness;

so that the needs and problems out of which they arise and which they have to satisfy be acknowledged. Secondly, that the secondary methods and conclusions be *brought back to the things of ordinary experience*, in all their coarseness and crudity, for verification. (1925, LW 1:39, my emphases)

His works often engage in this kind of genealogical analysis; see, for example, the discussion (and critique) of the origins of various philosophical conceptions in *Reconstruction in Philosophy*. Dewey embeds philosophy in broader culture and tries to uncover what philosophical conceptions might have done for human beings at particular stages of historical development, "study[ing] the history of philosophy not as an isolated thing but as a chapter in the development of civilization and culture" (1920, MW 12:93). Philosophies are seen as responses to the conditions and challenges of life at different historical junctures. What problems were philosophies devised to solve? Have they been successful? Have they created barriers to moving forward? Do new developments make revisions necessary? What dispositions did the old philosophies foster? Are these dispositions appropriate now, at this moment in history?

Dewey was, of course, a partisan reader of the philosophical tradition. Upon reflection, we might decide to reject some of his harsh verdicts. What seemed like unwarranted "acquiescence" to Dewey was, for Hegel, a way to "recognize the rose in the cross of the present and thereby to delight in the present."[17] What seemed to Dewey idle "flight from experience" may have been, for the Romantics, the only way of articulating their better hopes. The "attitude of control" he championed (1929, LW 4:81) isn't the only legitimate philosophical stance toward the world. Even by his own pragmatic standards, it can't be: different situations call for different attitudes. Philosophical irony, tragic insight, reverie, acceptance of the given—all have their place and time. The disposition Dewey favored in his critique of the tradition is appropriate in cases where we might still conceivably change things for the better; it is less appropriate when dealing with aspects of experience over which we have no control.

Whatever we think of his verdicts, Dewey gives us a valuable general insight. Instead of seeing philosophy "as so much nimble or severe intellectual exercise—as something said by philosophers and concerning them alone" (1916, MW 9:338), we should consider its effect on who we become. "Theory of education" now becomes an even richer field. It encompasses metaphilosophical critique.

Our portrait of Dewey as an educational theorist is now more nuanced. He wasn't just a kindly kindergarten reformer. He was also an original and provocative critic of the philosophical tradition who examined the way it has shaped us.

§1.7. PHILOSOPHICAL LABORATORY

The preceding discussion focused on how Dewey criticized traditional philosophies with respect to the "fundamental dispositions" to which they correspond. It focused on education broadly conceived. But this isn't the whole story. In Dewey's unorthodox approach, schools become testing grounds for philosophies. *Democracy and Education* tells us that philosophical conceptions should be "approached from the side of . . . the differences in educational practice they make when acted upon." This reveals their significance: "If a theory makes no difference in educational endeavor, it must be artificial" (1916, MW 9:338).

Dewey even says that "education is the laboratory in which philosophic distinctions become concrete and are tested" (1916,

MW 9:339). This "methodological centrality thesis" can be inter-
preted in different ways. It might refer to education broadly
conceived. It might also refer to schooling. Both approaches are
found in Dewey's works. Focusing on schooling makes sense in
light of Dewey's lifelong interest in formal education, including
not just schools but also kindergartens (1901, MW 1:230–37) and
colleges (1890, EW 3:51–55). This is especially true of *Democracy and Education*, where he offers the methodological centrality thesis. Much of the book is devoted to concrete classroom
problems. Should teachers focus on discipline at the expense of
interest? How much time should they devote to play? How
important are vocational skills? What is the value of teaching
students to enjoy their leisure? Can schools be made into "miniature communities" (1916, MW 9:370)?

In a bewildering way, the book constantly shifts between
addressing the schoolteacher's practical concerns ("Should I
include play time in the curriculum?") and raising large philosophical questions about the structure of experience, the origins
of education in early societies, even the nature of philosophy
itself. It's no surprise that Dewey isn't particularly popular. Those
who want practical teaching advice probably become impatient
at his forays into metaphilosophy; it's hard to imagine a schoolteacher getting excited about how philosophy should be defined,
yet Dewey spends an entire chapter on this question in *Democracy and Education*. Serious philosophers are likely to become
bored by Dewey's arguments about how geography should be
taught in schools, to which Dewey devotes another chapter in
that book. So they neglect him.

Tracing how *Democracy and Education* crosses between the
"practical" and the "abstract" levels reveals an underappreciated
aspect of the book. It shows us how Dewey envisages "testing"
philosophical conceptions "in educational endeavor" (1916, MW

9:338). Identifying problems—obstacles to human flourishing—is central to this process.

Dewey's work is remarkable for its sensitivity to "all that hems in and distorts human life" (1929–30, LW 5:297–98) and for his faith in gradually pushing back life's boundaries. *Democracy and Education* is justly famous for bringing to light how human experience can be distorted by defective schooling practices. It also seeks to identify the philosophical conceptions that underpin these problematic practices. The book's most provocative and famous conceptual revisions (reconceiving schools as "miniature communities," integrating vocational and liberal studies, and so on) occur precisely in this context.

Underlying Dewey's project in this book is the bold assumption that philosophies matter—they actually influence various practices. Traditional philosophical distinctions—labor and leisure, mind and matter, vocational and liberal arts, work and play—have all informed schooling, sometimes for the worse. They have resulted, for example, in a rigid separation between vocational and liberal schools, which, Dewey thinks, only helps exacerbate existing social divisions. He wants to challenge it and to imagine an alternative.

Recall the discussion of Dewey's philosophical method in §1.6. His "empirical method" is twofold: philosophical conceptions are "traced back to their origin in primary experience"; they are also "brought back to the things of ordinary experience, in all their coarseness and crudity, for verification" (1925, LW 1:39). Take the separation between liberal and vocational studies. Dewey looks at the philosophical assumptions that inform this practice. His genealogical critique seeks to show that they were informed by the rigid social divisions prevalent at the historical junctures when they were formulated: "These social ruptures of continuity were seen to have their intellectual formulation in

various dualisms and antitheses—such as that of labor and leisure, practical and intellectual activity" (1916, MW 9:332). All
this, he thinks, gave rise to the idea of "isolation of mind from
activity involving physical conditions" (1916, MW 9:333). But he
doesn't stop there. The other side of his philosophical method
is also at play. The conception of an isolated mind is "brought
back to the things of ordinary experience, in all their coarseness
and crudity, for verification" (1925, LW 1:39). How? By looking
at the effects it has on schooling. This is exactly what Dewey
does in *Democracy and Education*.

Throughout the book, he argues against the conception of
mind as isolated from physical activity. Why does he want to
revise this conception? In part, because of the scientific advances
that challenged it. But he is also worried that this conception of
mind hems in and distorts human experience when it's reflected
in schooling. He thinks that reconceiving the relationship
between mind and matter will help us develop better approaches
to intentionally organized education (1916, MW 9:343–55), a critique that goes hand in hand with that of the "spectator theories" of knowledge in *The Quest for Certainty*.

When schools rely on this conception of mind, knowledge
gained in the classroom is dead, "a mind-crushing load" (1916,
MW 9:159). Teachers who follow it fail to provide students with
knowledge that is alive and useful. The traditional conception
of mind fails Dewey's test: he believed that there can be no genuine learning without some active engagement with the material of one's experience. Corresponding to this criticism is the
idea that there is no such thing as a pure, disengaged knower,
since mind emerges in its interactions with the material and
social environment. That dead knowledge hems in human potential by creating alienated, passive, docile individuals who are
disengaged from their material and social environments. The

persons created by this system of formal education often lack autonomy; they're easy to take advantage of and to manipulate (1916, MW 9:159–60). A new philosophy is called for to remedy the situation.

So Dewey suggests that we view intelligence as a "purposive reorganization, through action, of the material of experience" and that we test this philosophical conception in schooling by implementing the concrete changes in educational method it implies (1916, MW 9:333). He hoped that this revision would enrich human experience by enhancing autonomy and creativity. This is an example of how philosophical conceptions, systems, and distinctions can be tested by the kinds of people—"the sort of individuals" (1920, MW 12:193)—they help create.

Taking the methodological centrality thesis seriously reveals new facets of Dewey's well-known masterpiece. He wasn't just giving good practical advice to teachers. He was also arguing for revising traditional philosophical conceptions (e.g. separation of mind and matter, spectator theories of knowledge) because they fail in educational practice. This also helps partially explain the bewildering back-and-forth between concrete problems of schooling and abstract philosophical debates. It wasn't just due to Dewey's eclectic interests. It was also (at least partially) motivated by his unorthodox view of philosophical methodology.

All this, of course, is consistent with the large program laid out earlier. Schooling is one of the institutions that is criticized in Dewey's sweeping project, which includes looking afresh at "every institution of the community" (1920, MW 12:193). But it has special importance: "When shall we realize that in every school-building in the land a struggle is also being waged against all that hems in and distorts human life?" (LW 5:1930, 297–98). Schooling shouldn't be neglected, since it's here that the foundations for a better society may be laid.

§1.8. CRITICISM AND IMAGINATION

The picture I have been painting is consistent with character-izations of philosophy we find elsewhere in Dewey's vast oeu-vre.[18] In *Experience and Nature*, philosophy is defined as "a critique of prejudices." Our "naive" experience of the world is overlaid with "interpretations, classifications" (1925, LW 1:40). These unexamined, often unconscious, habits of thinking may form barriers to growth in different spheres of life. Philosophy is seen as "a criticism of criticisms" (1925, LW 1:298–99) that aims to improve special disciplines, practices, and institutions. It helps facilitate human development.

In Dewey's program, criticism isn't pursued for its own sake. It's not supposed to end in a sophisticated aporia. It seeks to make life better. The aim isn't solving problems in theory. It's solving problems in practice. When Dewey writes that philosophy, like all thinking, is hypothetical and prospective, he is implicitly sug-gesting that philosophy, by itself, does not solve problems. It only "gives us an idea of what is possible," "an assignment of something to be tried" (1916, MW 9:336) Philosophical criticism isn't just an intellectual game. It opens space for a creative remak-ing of the world. When experience is "overlaid" with preconcep-tions, the world may appear "closed": things have *this* meaning and not another meaning; they are classified in *this* way and not another way; they have *these* possibilities and not others. Being stuck in ingrained habits can prevent growth. Philosophy helps us overcome these obstacles. We embrace our responsibility for ourselves and for the world we live in. Dewey even connects this conception of philosophy with democracy: "A philosophy ani-mated by the strivings of men for democracy will construe lib-erty as meaning a universe in which there is real contingency and uncertainty, a world which is not all in, and never will be, a world which in some respect is incomplete and in the making, and which in these respects may be made this way or that according as men judge, prize, love and labor. To such a philosophy any notion of a perfect and complete reality, finished, existing always the same without regard to the vicissitudes of time, will be abhorrent" (1919, MW 11:50).

Democracy and Education carries out this project with respect to schooling. By attacking rigid distinctions (mind and matter, labor and leisure, work and play) and questioning the traditional conception of mind (1916, MW 9:333), Dewey seeks to dislodge ingrained habits, paving way for better schooling. The book identifies specific classroom problems (e.g., apathy, isolation) and revises teaching methods to enhance human flourishing. It does this in the interest of facilitating education in its broadest sense—human development.

Philosophy isn't just all "negative" critique. It also involves imagining new possibilities. The two tasks are complementary. Criticism is not enough to facilitate human development; new directions for growth also have to be imagined, new institutions and practices devised. In "Philosophy and Democracy," Dewey even defines philosophy as "an intellectualized wish, an aspiration subjected to rational discrimination and tests, a social hope reduced to a working program of action, a prophecy of the future" (1919 MW 11:43). The connection between criticism and imagination, the one "negative" and the other "positive" (1920, MW 12:155), is clearly recognized in *The Quest for Certainty*:

Its philosophy's critical mind would be directed against the domination exercised by prejudice, narrow interest, routine custom and the authority which issues from institutions apart from the human ends they serve. This negative office would be but the obverse of the creative work of the imagination in pointing to the new possibilities which knowledge of the actual discloses and in projecting methods for their realization in the homely everyday experience of mankind. (1929, LW 4:248–49)

Democracy and Education deserves its fame for the innovative teaching methods it puts forward. "Bookish" studies should be connected to life; schools should become "miniature communities" where learning is a matter of sympathetic communication and cooperative pursuits (1916, MW 9:370). Dewey's imaginative theory of education seeks to foster genuine democracy. It is indeed "a social hope reduced to a working program of action" (1919 MW 11:43).

Human development requires that we imagine possibilities based on knowledge of actual facts, not mere wishful thinking. It also requires that we recognize new options disclosed by recent scientific discoveries. Hence, philosophy is also "a liaison officer between the conclusions of science and the modes of social and personal action through which attainable possibilities are projected and striven for" (1929, LW 4:248). Philosophy should try to connect our aspirations to the findings of modern science (1916, MW 9:339). *Democracy and Education* does this when it reimagines learning in light of new developments in evolutionary biology and psychology.

Now we have a coherent picture of Dewey's theory of education.

Still, no portrait is complete without criticism.

§1.9. EMPOWERING INTELLIGENCE

At its most ambitious, Dewey's philosophy of education is about investigating and facilitating human development. The far-reaching undertaking might raise eyebrows. Who are philosophers to help in this project? What right does philosophy have to tell us what education "in its largest sense" (1930, LW 5:289) might look like? In schools, Dewey tells us, "*we* may produce a projection in type of the society *we* should like to realize, and by forming minds in accord with it gradually modify the larger and more recalcitrant features of adult society" (1916, MW 9:326, my emphases). Who are the "we" in this sentence?

These questions take us back to Plato's *Republic*. They arise with particular force with respect to the Simple Platonist's educational project. (Here I will follow Dewey in taking Plato's suggestions in the *Republic* at face value, which is obviously not the only way to read it.) The book is so provocative because it is, by turns, both seductive and horrifying. There's no denying it's enticing—"a splendid and imperishable vision" (1888, EW 1:240–41). If only we knew the ideal way to live, if only we could prepare everyone to fit into the perfect pattern! It is also deeply unsettling. To implement the "splendid" vision, the city would take "every precaution to ensure that no mother knows her own child."[19] And this in service of the ideal way of life as conceived by philosophers (one might also say: *for* philosophers, since it ranks the philosophical life highest). Education is conceived as a tool to institute the Good as understood by a small intellectual elite. Clearly, mothers weren't asked for their opinion on these proposals.

Is Dewey's large-scale undertaking also suspect? It seems so: "philosophic theory has no Aladdin's lamp to summon into immediate existence the values which it internally constructs. . . . By the educative arts philosophy *may generate methods of utilizing the energies of human beings* in accord with serious and thoughtful conceptions of life" (1916, MW 9:339, my emphasis).

Dewey's phrasing doesn't help his cause. "Utilize the energies of human beings?" Do those whose energies are "utilized" have to consent to this? By what standards are success and failure to be judged? What are the costs of various social experiments, including those in education? What authority does philosophy have to suggest "conceptions of life" to be tried?

Dewey even used the phrase "social engineering" (1920, MW 12:179). Clearly, he saw schools as sites for social experimentation. He called them "philosophical laboratories" (1916, MW 9:339). But he never told us how exactly the experiments he advocated would be conducted. Who would be put in charge? How would potential costs be assessed and dealt with? When discussing moral experimentation, Dewey writes: "Mistakes are no longer either mere unavoidable accidents to be mourned or moral sins to be expiated and forgiven. They are *lessons* in wrong methods of using intelligence and instructions as to a better course in the future" (1920, MW 12:180, my emphasis).

To be sure, mistakes in social experimentation might reveal valuable insights. But they also have costs. When he suggests that they aren't to be seen as "mere unavoidable accidents to be mourned" or as "moral sins," Dewey's tone seems to be too cavalier. How do we weigh the benefits of learning from mistakes on our way "to a better course in the future" against the human suffering they may cause?

This worry reveals a gap in Dewey's thought. His great ambition was to offer us a robust methodology for making social progress. He didn't fully develop it. (Of course, this doesn't mean it can't be done.)[20] The talk of "testing" gives his philosophy of education a deceptive air of precision. He didn't tell us what counts as success and failure. Philosophy of education, as it is elaborated in Dewey's oeuvre, is ambitious yet incomplete. "Is education really possible, means: Is it possible to apply intelligence intentionally and systematically to the regulation of life?" (1930, LW 5:290) The question Dewey attributed to the Ancients is still with us.

Another worry has to do with the philosopher's role in this process. The passage quoted earlier conjures up a troubling image. Philosophy "internally constructs" (1916, MW 9:339) conceptions of the good life and then "tests" them on potentially unwilling subjects in schools.

A full response to this worry will have to wait until the next chapter, where Dewey's understanding of the connection between democracy and inquiry will be explained. But we can anticipate it. The discussion in §1.3 already hints at some of the resources Dewey has to mitigate the worry (at least partially). Unlike Simple Platonism, Deweyan philosophy of education isn't about formulating a complete, once-and-for-all account of the good life. It's about helping prepare individuals to take an active part in the process of figuring out how they should live.

This inquiry spans the entire democratic community. Schooling should empower human beings to take charge of their personal and social growth. Dewey dreamed of a world where "there is a responsible share on the part of each person, in proportion to capacity, in shaping the aims and policies of the social group to which he belongs" (1920, MW 12:199).

The phrasing of the passages I quoted earlier (where Dewey suggests that philosophy "internally constructs" values and conceptions of the good life, 1916, MW 9:339) is unfortunate. It doesn't reflect his view that inquiry is a "cooperative effort" (1929, LW 4:250) and that it should include a wide range of perspectives. Dewey even singled out communication as an important "test" for conceptions of goods: "Indeed, capacity to endure publicity and communication is the test by which it is decided whether a pretended good is genuine or spurious" (1920, MW 12:197). In *Experience and Nature*, he writes:

> Its [philosophy's] business is to accept and to utilize for a purpose the best available knowledge of its own time and place. And this purpose is the criticism of beliefs, institutions, customs, policies with respect to their bearing upon good. This does not mean their bearing upon *the* good, as something itself attained and formulated in philosophy. For . . . philosophy . . . has no private access to good. . . . it accepts the goods that are diffused in human experience. It has no Mosaic or Pauline authority of revelation entrusted to it. But it has the authority of intelligence, of criticism of these common and natural goods. (1925, LW 1:305, my emphasis)

This implies that philosophers should engage with other members of their communities in a wider project of inquiry into values. Philosophers play a special role not because they have some "private" access to "the good" but because they can subject the goods recognized by others to criticism. This brings to mind, by contrast, Aristotle's vivid description of the popular reaction to Plato's lectures: "Everyone came expecting they would acquire one of *the sorts of thing people normally regard as good* . . . they came looking for some wonderful kind of happiness. But when the discussion turned out to be about mathematics, about numbers and geometry and astronomy, and then, to cap it all, he claimed that the Good is One, it seemed to them, I imagine, something utterly paradoxical. The result was that some of them sneered at the lecture, and others were full of reproaches."[21] Dewey's approach was radically different. He wouldn't have perplexed an audience eager for happiness with a discussion of geometry and astronomy. When Dewey did lecture, he appealed to his audience's deeply held values: the belief in the importance of individuality, in "the democratic way of life," in "freedom and cooperative peace" (1941, LW 14:262–65). These ideas weren't meant to be paradoxical in the least.

Does this make Dewey a conventional, boring philosopher? I think not. For Dewey was, despite appealing to commonly held values, deeply critical of the status quo. He sought to point out how the current arrangements fall short of the values we ourselves profess; to identify inconsistencies in our outlook; to propose ways to realize one of humanity's highest hopes: making "a life worth living" (1920, MW 12:200–201) open to all human beings. His faith in democracy didn't entail a naive acceptance of the status quo but instead served as a basis for criticizing the institutions of his time and imagining how democracy may be more fully realized.

This might partially mitigate the worry about the philosopher's role. Dewey didn't seek to put forward some utterly paradoxical view of the good. Nor did he think of the philosopher as "revealing" truths from above. He tried to take the enterprise forward by pointing out how our current arrangements fall short of what we profess, by exploring what our values really mean and exact of us, if taken seriously. This becomes clear when he discusses the modern American commitments to democracy and individuality. As Dewey saw it, despite paying lip service to the idea of individuality, contemporary capitalist America instead stifles it by assigning the mass of human beings to unfulfilling jobs and using standardized educational approaches that foster mediocrity (see 1922, MW 13:289–300). The Deweyan philosopher is merely a facilitator. The community articulates its goals by engaging in democratic dialogue. Individuals aren't to be mere passive participants in this process. Deweyan schooling seeks to put them in charge.

Simple Platonism envisages giving the philosopher absolute authority to formulate and institute the Good, once and for all. On Dewey's view, empowering intelligence has an entirely different meaning. It means empowering individual human beings to engage in articulating the meanings, values and ends of their existence in sympathetic, open-minded (and open-ended) dialogue with one another. Even in his conception of philosophy, Dewey was a democrat (1925, LW 1:305).

§1.10. THE AMERICAN OPTIMIST

Dewey conceived of theory of education as facilitating a large-scale project of human development. This is an optimistic enterprise. It is based on faith in the possibility of improvement. It's also based on faith in philosophy's positive, constructive, forward-looking role. In conceiving of philosophy this way, Dewey was a quintessential optimist.

He once said that philosophies are "organized ways of living" (1916, MW 9:334). Pragmatism is a way of life, too. Unlike Hegelianism, it doesn't seek "reconciliation" by looking back at history to discern "the rational in the actual."[22] Unlike stoicism, it doesn't find tranquility by embracing fate. Chrysippus's favorite phrase, "Therefore accept whatever evil or good he [Zeus] may send to each of you,"[23] distills the attitude that pragmatism rejects. It looks to the future, not the past. It sees us living in a world without predetermined outcomes (1919, MW 11:50). Instead of accepting "whatever evil" we face, pragmatism hopes to improve life.

Philosophy in itself doesn't bring us reconciliation. It doesn't have that kind of power. Like all thinking, it is hypothetical and prospective—"an assignment of something to be tried" (1916, MW 9:336).[24] It can bring to light how our experience is "hemmed in" (1929–30, LW 5:297–98) by the existing arrangements. It can also offer us tentative hypotheses about how the various "shifting scenes" of life might be connected. It can suggest how we might change our individual and communal habits in order to lead richer lives. In an uncertain world, philosophy is prospective. Its mission is not to reconcile us with the world, but to help us remake it.

When reading Dewey, it is impossible to avoid worrying that he was too optimistic. Harsher critics might say he was naive. This is a question about the "temper" of Dewey's thought. It's fair to raise it. After all, to do so is to use Dewey's own favorite strategy—assessing philosophies with respect to the "fundamental dispositions" they encourage (see 1920, MW 12:135, and 1925, LW 1:326).

Dewey was certainly an optimist, but he was neither naive nor simple-minded. This is an important qualification. Perhaps we can talk of different varieties of optimism.

"Panglossian" optimism ignores or explains away suffering. This certainly wasn't Dewey's stance. He was a perceptive critic of the boundaries that hem in human lives: the drudgery of industrial capitalism, the apathy of overly authoritative classrooms, the way prejudices based on race, sex, or class confine us. As a social critic, Dewey showed deep sensitivity to human suffering. Alan Ryan captures the "temper" of his philosophy beautifully when he writes: "Dewey was unique in the way he combined fierce criticism of the particulars of human existence with a resounding endorsement of the human project."[25]

"Blind" optimism refuses to admit the possibility of failure. Was Dewey too naive about the likelihood of realizing our "highest hopes?" Was his emphasis on taking "control" of human development arrogant? Did he ignore our limitations?

With this, too, Dewey can't be charged. A careful reading reveals his humility:

> A mind that has opened itself to experience and that has ripened through its discipline knows its own littleness and impotencies; it knows that its own wishes and acknowledgements are not final measures of the universe whether in knowledge or in conduct, and hence are, in the end, transient. But it also knows that its juvenile assumption of power and achievement is not a dream to be wholly forgotten. . . . A chastened sense of our importance, apprehension that it is not a yard-stick by which to measure the whole, is consistent with the belief that we and our endeavors are significant not only for themselves but in the whole. (1925, LW 1:313–14)

The world resists us. Dewey recognized this.[26] That is why the opening pages of *Democracy and Education* characterize growth as learning that occurs when dealing with the world's disruptive, challenging features. Our wishes aren't its "final measure." Dewey even calls the assumption of power and achievement "juvenile," which is particularly striking in view of his defense of "the attitude of control" (1929, LW 4:81). The vision offered here is nuanced. It may be "juvenile" to go on this assumption, but it is "not a dream to be wholly forgotten." Why?

Underpinning Dewey's pragmatism is a special view of the human predicament. Grasping it illuminates his version of optimism. The universe is neither wholly hostile nor wholly hospitable. Nature offers us a "peculiar intermixture of support and frustration" (1925, LW 1:314). Dewey's optimism doesn't assume complete harmony. Nor does it assume permanent alienation. It aims to help human beings gradually learn from the world and contribute to its development. Like his fellow pragmatist William James, Dewey believed our efforts "carry the universe forward" (1925, LW 1:214). This mixture of humility about our limits and faith in our significance is characteristic of the temper of his thought.

The closing pages of *Experience and Nature* express this humble optimism. Dewey is careful to point out that to believe in his project "is not to assert that intelligence will ever dominate the course of events; it is not even to imply that it will save from ruin and destruction" (1925, LW 1:326). His vision is hypothetical. Its worth can't be determined by argument alone. It should be tested in experience. "Wholesale triumph" isn't guaranteed:

> The issue is one of choice, and choice is always a question of alternatives. What the method of intelligence, thoughtful valuation will accomplish, if once it be tried, is for the result of trial to determine. . . . Faith in a wholesale and final triumph is fantastic. But some procedure has to be tried; for life is itself a sequence of trials. Carelessness and routine, Olympian aloofness, secluded contemplation are themselves choices. . . . These procedures have been tried and have worked their will. . . . But this conception of philosophy also waits to be tried. (1925, LW 1:326)

Dewey was neither a "Panglossian" nor a "blind" optimist. His brand of pragmatic optimism actually comes with a provocative insight. Pessimism and acquiescence can become self-fulfilling prophecies. Philosophies that embrace reconciliation with pain and suffering may obscure possibilities for improving life. This was precisely Dewey's charge against traditional philosophies.

They prejudged the case. When advocating acquiescence, abnegation or "flight from the hardships of life" (1925, LW 1:325), they created a self-fulfilling prophecy: "No one knows how many of the evils and deficiencies that are pointed to as reasons for flight from experience *are themselves due* to the disregard of experience shown by those peculiarly reflective" (1925, LW 1:41, my emphasis). To prejudge our efforts to improve existence as doomed to failure is to abandon our responsibility to shape it.

I will call a third version of optimism "the optimism of wholeness." Dewey was guilty of it. Although he rejected Hegelian acquiescence, in one sense he forever remained Hegel's faithful disciple. Dewey sought wholeness and reconciliation of the opposites—if not in thinking, then in life. Whenever he encountered "dualisms and antagonisms," his strategy was *always* to try to overcome them. This is acknowledged in his autobiography: "the demand for unification . . . was doubtless *an intense emotional craving*. . . . The sense of divisions and separations that were, I suppose, borne in upon me as a consequence of a heritage of New England culture, divisions by way of isolation of self from world, of soul from body, of nature from God, brought a painful oppression—or, rather, they were an inward laceration" (1930, LW 5:153, my emphasis).

As a result, his works often underplay genuine tensions. After all, not all dualisms are mere obstacles. Some might actually be useful; some might track features of experience that might be difficult (if not impossible) to eradicate.[27] For instance, Dewey dreamed of a world where the divisions between work and play, the aesthetic and the ordinary would disappear. Then "the hardness and crudeness of contemporary life will be bathed in the light that never was on land or sea" (1920, MW 12:200–201). It is hard not to see this as overly optimistic. While challenging these "dualisms" can be helpful, it is unlikely that the intense "demand for unification" (which he himself acknowledged to be an "emotional craving") can be fully met.

This doesn't mean we should reject his project. "The optimism of wholeness," while characteristic of his writings, isn't essential to the enterprise. He can be taken seriously for suggesting potential sites of improvement; we need not follow him in always seeking harmony.

§1.11. A NEW PORTRAIT

It troubled Dewey that philosophers ignored his work on education: "Although a book called *Democracy and Education* was for many years that in which my philosophy, such as it was, was most fully expounded, I do not know that philosophic critics, as distinct from teachers, have ever had recourse to it" (1930, LW 5:156). He even said he would have preferred to have been criticized for making education central to his thought, instead of being utterly dismissed: "I can recall but one critic who has suggested that my thinking has been too much permeated by interest in education. . . . At all events, this handle is offered to any subsequent critic who may wish to lay hold of it" (1930, LW 5:156).

The situation hasn't improved that much since Dewey's time. Teachers still read his theory of education; philosophers pass it by. Certainly, a vast number of Dewey studies have been written, Alan Ryan's perceptive book *John Dewey and the High Tide of American Liberalism* among them. Still, no philosophical commentary takes Dewey's focus on education seriously; none explains how it was central to his thought. The common portrait of Dewey as a philosopher of education is that of a kindly "progressive" reformer who wasn't a particularly deep or interesting philosopher, a view I hope to correct.

The different pieces of the puzzle—Dewey's odd claims about the substantive and the methodological importance of education to philosophy—now fit together. At its most general, "theory of education" is about investigating and facilitating human development in the interest of enhancing flourishing (§1.2–3). Schooling is an important tool for advancing this project (§1.4). But the enterprise is even broader. All practices and institutions that shape who we become should be examined and improved (§1.5). Schools are among them (§1.7). Philosophy itself is subjected to Dewey's searching analysis—with education as the touchstone (§1.6 and §1.7).

Now we are finally in a position to appreciate just how rich, varied, and significant philosophy of education can be. We are also starting to get a fresh portrait of Dewey as an educational theorist. A full picture will require looking at how his other works—such as *Art as Experience* and "Creative Democracy"—fit into the program I have been outlining.

2

DEMOCRACY AND EDUCATION

§2.1. RENEWING THE TRADITION

After the violence at the Capitol on January 6, 2021, it has become blatantly clear that American democracy is under threat. To say we should turn to philosophy at this pivotal moment is to invite scornful laughter. The challenges we face surely go far beyond philosophy's powers. And, perhaps, philosophy can offer us only reasons for despair. Had he watched the attack on the Capitol, Plato wouldn't have been surprised. Democracy "breeds anarchy." It degenerates into tyranny. This happens when "a democratic city, athirst for freedom, happens to get bad cupbearers for its leaders." Eventually it gets "a leader . . . who dominates a docile mob and doesn't restrain himself from spilling kindred blood."[1] Walter Lippmann, Plato's self-styled modern disciple, warned more than a century ago that democracies are bound to be blinded by stereotypes and propaganda.[2] Faith in democracy seemed to him utterly naive.

At this decisive point in our history, dispiriting skepticism isn't all philosophy has to offer. A brighter story can be found in the writings of America's great democrat. Dewey understood full well that critics like Lippmann raise serious worries. He called

Lippmann's criticisms "perhaps the most effective indictment of democracy as currently conceived ever penned" (1922, MW 13:337). Still, he held on to his unwavering belief in democracy. He did so for almost a century, arguing against democracy's foes—domestic skeptics, foreign dictators, radicals who wanted to achieve their ends by "undemocratic means" (1937, LW 11:298)—and, of course, philosophers who sneered at democratic optimism.[3]

Was Dewey merely a naive apologist for American democracy, with all its imperfections? Was he clear-eyed about our problems, but too headstrong to admit defeat in the face of arguments the force of which he recognized? Simple-minded celebration of the status quo wasn't Dewey's aim. Detractors of democracy challenged him to think hard about its meaning and ideals: "The old saying that the cure for the ills of democracy is more democracy . . . may also indicate the need of returning to the idea itself, of clarifying and deepening our apprehension of it, and of employing our sense of its meaning to criticize and remake its political manifestations." Some criticisms, he conceded, "are only too well grounded" (1927, LW 2:325). Expressing democratic ideals afresh, scrutinizing our current practices, suggesting ways of improving them to realize our "better hopes" (1916, MW 9:85)—that was his project. Enhancing democracy, not excusing its current failings. His work on democratic education was an essential part of that enterprise.

"Lack of confidence in the democratic way of life" isn't a new sentiment. In 1941, Dewey addressed young people disillusioned by joblessness and insecurity. What did he tell them? "Democracy is a moving thing. . . . Its possibilities are far from exhausted." Democracy is a project in the making. Don't judge it too hastily by its current failures. We democratic citizens can still make it better. Dewey wanted to give his anxious audience "a sense of unrealized possibilities opening new horizons which will inspire them to creative effort . . . the sense of something fine and great for which to live" (1941, LW 14:263).

"The sense of something fine and great for which to live." Nothing could be further from the thin view that merely tolerates democracy as the "least bad" set of institutions. In fact, Dewey didn't think democracy was merely a matter of the organization and institutions of government. He thought of it as a culture, a way of life for which we are personally responsible: "Democracy is a *personal* way of individual life. . . . It signifies the possession and continual use of certain attitudes, forming personal character and determining desire and purpose in all the relations of life" (1939, LW 14:226). Democracy is more than government. It is an ethos. "Without this basis, it [government] is worth nothing. A gust of prejudice, a blow of despotism, and it falls like a card house" (1888, EW 1:240). And his life's work was directed as much at dealing with abstract concepts—experience, inquiry, growth—as it was at promoting that ethos. To be sure, he addressed philosophers. But he also addressed those who, like the young people in his 1941 audience, felt lost, anxious, disillusioned.

He told them there's still work to be done. We shouldn't act as if "our ancestors had succeeded in setting up a machine that solved the problem of perpetual motion in politics" (1939, LW 14:225). Institutions by themselves won't magically realize all of our hopes and keep democracy safe for us forever. There is no room for complacency.[4] This hard lesson Dewey learned by witnessing the rise of totalitarianism in his lifetime. Reflecting on its menace in 1939, he wrote that "powerful present enemies of democracy can be successfully met only by the creation of personal attitudes in individual human beings" (1939, LW 14:226). The idea is echoed in another essay, "I Believe," where Dewey writes that democratic individuals "are the sole final warrant for the existence and endurance of democratic institutions" (1939, LW 14:92). Part of the answer lies in every individual's hands. Another part requires large-scale efforts. Reforming education to improve our democratic culture is crucial. A 1934 essay, "The Need for a Philosophy of Education," offers a prescient diagnosis of the problems that still plague us:

> The other especially urgent need is connected with the present unprecedented wave of nationalistic sentiment, of racial and national prejudice, of readiness to resort to force of arms. For this spirit to have arisen on such a scale the schools must have somehow failed grievously. . . . We now know the enemy; it is out in the open. Unless the schools of the world can unite in effort to rebuild the spirit of common understanding, of mutual sympathy and goodwill among all peoples and races, to exorcise the demon of prejudice, isolation and hatred, they themselves are likely to be submerged by the general return to barbarism, the sure outcome of present tendencies if unchecked by the forces which education alone can evoke and fortify. (1934, LW 9:203–4)

Taking Dewey's proposal seriously means renewing the tradition of seeing education as central to political philosophy. In a 1941 address, "Lessons from the War—in Philosophy," Dewey took a hard look at the modern state of the ancient discipline. What lessons can philosophers draw from the rise of totalitarianism in Nazi Germany? That they should stop neglecting "the most urgent problem of *education in its broadest and deepest sense*: The formation of the attitudes and dispositions in human beings. . . . For the habits formed decide in the long run . . . the kind of customs and institutions which come to prevail socially" (1941, LW 14:323, my emphasis).

What lessons can philosophy draw from democracy's ongoing troubles, so vividly exemplified by the attack on the Capitol on January 6, 2021? We should take seriously the age-old project of thinking about the relationship between democracy, character, and education.[5] The task is critical for safeguarding the democratic way of life. To say the discipline should play a role in strengthening democracy is to reveal one's optimistic faith in its ability to improve existence. Some sages seek instead to rise above our worldly troubles. No one has captured philosophy's seductive offer of seclusion from the "madness" and "lawlessness" of public life more eloquently than did Socrates in the *Republic*:

> The members of this small group [philosophers] have tasted how sweet and blessed a possession philosophy is, and at the same time they've also seen the madness of the majority and realized. . . . They would perish before they could profit either their city or their friends and be useless both to themselves and to others. . . . Taking all this into account, they lead a quiet life and do their own work. Thus, like someone who takes refuge under a little wall from a storm of dust or hail driven by the wind, the philosopher—seeing others filled with lawlessness—is satisfied if he can somehow lead his present life free from injustice and impious acts.[6]

There might be moments in history when nothing else is left. Perhaps Plato's was such a time. Ours isn't. "Seeing others filled with lawlessness," philosophy shouldn't hide "from a storm of dust or hail driven by the wind" in abstruse speculation, waiting until it, too, is swept away.

It should take democratic education seriously.

But what exactly does this entail? A superficial view of the field sees it as elaborating some version of a boring, simplistic thesis: "Teaching 'civics' is important." This seems thin compared to the weighty issues that lie at the "core" of political thought, such as the nature of justice, the proper limits of liberty, the legitimacy of state power. Sure, teaching "civics," creating an "informed electorate," perhaps even cultivating a few virtues may help us strengthen democracy. But all this doesn't seem particularly deep or philosophically interesting. So the issue of democratic education remains largely at the discipline's periphery. Teachers may care about it; philosophers mostly don't.[7]

In his pioneering work on democratic education, Dewey shows philosophers an alternative to their "closeted seclusion" (1930, LW 5:297). This doesn't mean focusing on superficial topics. The field isn't just about "civics."[8] The questions he considered within his expansive theory of democratic education are as big as any philosophy has ever asked.

How do our social arrangements, the public cultures we belong to, shape us? Are we responsible for shaping them? Should the relationship be improved? Can we set up a virtuous circle, so that our social arrangements and our personalities may be mutually enhanced? What role should schooling play in this ambitious project? These questions are about "education in its largest sense" (1930, LW 5:289). They deal with the formation of our "fundamental dispositions, intellectual and emotional" (1916, MW 9:338–39). Obviously, they are rather general. But we can make them more concrete. We can raise them in specific social contexts. Plato did this in ancient Athens; Dewey—in twentieth-century America. Dewey admired Plato's insight in grasping the connection between politics and education, now largely overlooked: "It would be impossible to find in any scheme of philosophic thought other than Plato's a more adequate recognition on one hand of the educational significance of social arrangements and, on the other, of the dependence of those arrangements upon the means used to educate the young" (1916, MW 9:95).

Like Plato, Dewey reflected on both sides of the equation. But the real implications of his far-reaching vision of democratic education have been largely misunderstood and neglected.

Why bother reconstructing Dewey's account of education for and by democracy?[9] Deciphering his complex vision reveals the lines along which inquiry may proceed if we are to renew the great tradition of connecting education and politics (one that also includes Plato, Jean-Jacques Rousseau, and W. E. B. Du Bois, among others).[10] The enterprise isn't just of scholarly interest. Focusing on education can help us reorient reflections on political philosophy to questions of central importance for our troubled times.

§2.2. THE HALL OF DEMOCRATIC PERSONALITIES

Running through the philosophical tradition of taking education seriously is a longstanding conversation about "democratic individuals" (1939, LW 14:92). It examines the human beings who sustain democracy and are, in turn, shaped by it. Plato's scathing critique is familiar: incapable of discriminating between conflicting appetites, the democratic character of his time yielded "day by day to the desire at hand," "saying and doing whatever comes into his mind. . . . There's neither order nor necessity in his life."[11] Plato seems to have liked stable, harmonious characters ruled by reason (a type exemplified so unforgettably by Socrates). He held the vacillating, "lawless" democratic self in contempt. The culture of Athenian democracy, too, was condemned: it led even the best citizens astray. Shaped by that ethos, they chased honor, riches, and appetitive gratification, neglecting the highest part of their souls—reason. In that milieu, even the best led "lives that are inappropriate and untrue."[12] Dewey saw democracy as "forming personal character" (1939, LW 14:226). Plato wouldn't have disagreed. Sure, democracy forms character. That's precisely why he condemned it.[13]

Rousseau called the *Republic* "the most beautiful educational treatise ever written." But, he continued, the ancient vision of public education "denatures" human beings, sacrificing the individual's "original" inclinations for unqualified adherence to public duty.[14] For all its flaws, such as the highly sexist education of Sophie, Rousseau's response to Plato, *Emile*, stands as a lasting tribute to the value of autonomy. Its democratic education seeks to create human beings who combine autonomy with affection, freedom—with fellowship. Emile doesn't seek to dominate others. He is prepared to live with them on equal terms, in peace: "The spirit of peace is an effect of his education which . . . has diverted him from seeking his pleasures in domination and in another's unhappiness."[15]

Dewey adds to the debate. He gives us yet another picture to add to the hall of democratic personalities. In some ways, he inherited Rousseau's educational project: to cultivate a combination of autonomy and sympathy, to develop both independent thinking and affective ties between citizens. In other ways he went beyond it, adding a modern twist by focusing his program of education on "the evolution of conscious life" (1916, MW 9:369). Rousseau's Emile is quite conventional. Not so the Deweyan creative self. This democratic personality is interested in improving our individual and collective habits to enhance human flourishing. It seeks to take an active part in the reshaping of the world, "a world which is not all in, and never will be, a world which in some respect is incomplete and in the making, and which in these respects may be made this way or that according as men judge, prize, love and labor" (1919, MW 11:50).

Talk about "democratic character" may sound misleading. It links dramatically different accounts in a superficially unified story: Plato's critique of the "lawless" characters of his fellow Athenians, Rousseau's Romantic eighteenth-century vision, Dewey's modern pragmatist program. In a sense, of course, they were talking about different things. Athenian democracy in 375 BCE and American democracy in 1916 were thousands of years apart. But these thinkers were in conversation with each other. Rousseau responded to Plato's *Republic*, Dewey to both Plato's *Republic* and Rousseau's *Emile*. As he pondered the goals of education—good citizenship and natural development—Dewey reflected on the debate between his predecessors. He even mused about Plato's hidden influence on Rousseau (1916, MW 9:97). The notion of "democratic individuals" helps us examine this dialogue, still essential in our times.

Who are the Deweyan "democratic individuals" (1939, LW14:92)? No single place in Dewey's works captures the whole picture. Which doesn't mean he had nothing serious to say about it. In fact, this was one of the dominant themes of his remarkably long career.

Already in 1888, the young Dewey linked democracy to personal development (1888, EW 1:244). In the ensuing decades, he abandoned many of his early commitments. The Hegelian organicism of his youth eventually gave way to a growing appreciation of individuality.[16] Darwin and William James inspired Dewey to replace his religious view of selfhood with naturalistic psychology. As he matured, his beliefs shifted. But the connection between democracy and personal growth remained constant.

In 1916, Dewey published a book on how schooling might facilitate the co-development of democratic personalities and democratic cultures. *Democracy and Education* (1916, MW 9) became his most famous work. The year 1920 saw the publication of his pragmatic manifesto *Reconstruction in Philosophy*. It advocated realizing the "moral meaning" of democracy: "to set free and to develop the capacities of human individuals without respect to race, sex, class or economic status" (1920, MW 12:186). A response to skepticism about the democratic public— *The Public and Its Problems*—was published seven years later. It, too, talked about the "liberation of the potentialities" of democratic citizens (1927, LW 2:328). "Creative Democracy" argued that democratic dialogue enriches our personalities (1939, LW 14:228).

It isn't easy to get a clear-cut account of "democratic individuals" from all these writings. The story has to be carefully reconstructed from a number of disparate remarks. But the effort is worth the trouble. For Dewey was one of our foremost theorists of democratic education. He spent almost a century thinking about the link between democracy and personal growth. To be sure, there are loose strands in his vast picture, for example, his appeal to "native energies" and "irreducible uniqueness" in the account of how the personality develops. But there are also insights that address present-day disenchantment, insights that haven't yet been fully appreciated.

How might democracy shape us? How might we shape it? What form of life, what sort of human experience, goes hand in hand with taking part in a democratic culture? Plato's answer was grim. Dewey's wasn't. His life's work was devoted to defending the goodness and the grace of democratic character.

§2.3. THE EVOLUTION OF
CONSCIOUS LIFE

Dewey's most famous book, *Democracy and Education*, provides a good starting point for reconstructing his portrait of the "democratic individual." The book tells us she's a growing personality that contributes to the growth of her community: "a character which . . . is interested in the continuous readjustment . . . essential to growth" (1916, MW 9:370).[17] But what exactly is "growth"? Elucidating this is crucial for grasping the true nature of Dewey's vision.[18]

Pick up any book or essay from Dewey's thirty-seven-volume oeuvre, and chances are it will mention "growth" at some point. In *Democracy and Education* he used the term to define genuine education, to set the aim of formal schooling, to describe the outcome of democratic dialogue and even to capture the distinguishing features of life. In *Art as Experience* it is used to illuminate the nature of aesthetic experience. In *Reconstruction in Philosophy* it becomes the focus of his pragmatic program. Still, it remains poorly understood. No commentary to date does justice to this central concept.[19] The trouble is, of course, that Dewey never produced a clear definition. The casual reader could be forgiven for thinking it's just an empty buzzword with little real philosophical significance.

But it is the key to Dewey's thought. In a response to one of his critics, Dewey indicated that what connects all his works is "the principle of development that holds so universally in my theory of a variety of phases of experience such as morals, politics, religion, science, philosophy itself, as well as the fine arts" (1949, LW 16:397). This principle is growth.

So what is it? To get the answer, we need to start by looking at the opening chapters of *Democracy and Education*. The notion makes its first appearance in the discussion of the fundamental features of all forms of life. Growth occurs when a living organism spends energy to make a re-adjustment in response to a disruption in its equilibrium (1916, MW 9:4). As the organism solves the problem it faces, it often changes its environment. Higher-level organisms also gain new habits that direct future activity (1916, MW 9:52). We are told that growth is progressive: "A possibility of progress is opened up by the fact that in learning one act, methods are developed good for use in other situations" (1916, MW 9:50). As organisms grow, they increase their capacities relative to their environments. They learn to deal with a wider range of challenging situations likely to arise for them (though there may be some losses).

The opening chapters of *Democracy and Education* give us resources to reconstruct part of the picture. But this is not enough. They only tell us about growth in its most general sense—as it applies to all forms of life. We don't yet learn how this picture translates to the realm of human conduct. Dewey clearly thought that it does translate to the human realm. The opening pages of *Democracy and Education* paint a sweeping picture of the *continuity* between all forms of life. And, of course, the book constantly appeals to "growth" in the educational context.

To grasp all this we need to look elsewhere. We have already been told that growth for higher-level organisms involves a modification of habits. This is the central subject of *Human Nature and Conduct*. Here we find more resources to put together Dewey's picture of human development. The first step is to appreciate the importance he accorded to habits. Whether we recognize this or not, our conduct is largely governed by habits (although we can revise them). Our virtues and vices are habits. Habits affect our sensations, ideas, and thoughts (1922, MW 14:25). They help define our characters (1922, MW 14:21, 29). Where do our habits come from? Prior adjustments to the environment.

Dewey's attitude to the influence of habits on human conduct was complex. Habits can be helpful. They allow us to act more efficiently (1922, MW 14:121). Habits let us go on "autopilot" when performing routine tasks. This frees us up for dealing with the new problems that constantly confront us. But blindly following fixed habits yields suboptimal results. *Art as Experience* laments the numbing effects of "routine" habit on aesthetic perception: "Familiarity induces indifference, prejudice blinds us; conceit looks through the wrong end of a telescope. . . . Art throws off the covers that hide the expressiveness of experienced things; it quickens us from the slackness of routine and enables us to forget ourselves by finding ourselves in the delight of experiencing the world about us in varied qualities and forms" (1934, LW 10:110).

Familiarity makes us insensitive to the beauty of life. Worse still, conceit and prejudice confine us. Though his account of this is unsophisticated by today's standards, Dewey was deeply concerned about racial prejudice, a "social disease" we should eradicate (1922, MW 13:242–43). He saw prejudices as defective habits that should be revised (1922, MW 13:244).

In general, Dewey believed that no single set of habits will secure a permanent adjustment to the ever-changing environment (1922, MW 14:38). New challenges keep arising. New facets of experience wait to be explored. Problems to which we had hitherto been numb must be confronted. Constant revision is necessary. There can be no fixed, stable, perfect character of the sort the Simple Platonist seeks.

In his account of deliberation (the intelligent revision of habits) in *Human Nature and Conduct*, Dewey tells us that revising habits shapes character (1992, MW 14:132). This yields a new gloss on Deweyan growth. When it comes to individuals, growth is a process of character-formation in which the individual reshapes her habits so as to develop her capacities to deal with a wider range of challenging situations likely to arise for her. The process may also involve making changes in her environment.

Deweyan growth isn't supposed to be selfish or short-sighted. It involves an intelligent revision of habits (individual and collective) in light of an open-minded, sympathetic, responsible, and imaginative survey of their consequences (1916, MW 9:127; 1922, MW 14:144; 1922, MW 14:169). When it comes to the kind of growth that involves specifically this type of deliberation, communication with others becomes particularly important, since we may not fully appreciate how individual and collective habits affect other human beings prior to engaging with them. This kind of conversation lies at the heart of Deweyan democracy.

A contrast with Rousseau's *Emile* helps clarify this crucial point. Rousseau conceived of "conscience" as an originally given "voice of nature" that delivers the verdict without the need to engage in dialogue with others. Listen to your heart, and you will hear the answer: "I have only to consult myself about what I want to do. Everything I sense to be good is good; Everything I sense to be bad is bad. The best of all casuists is the conscience."[20] This is the antithesis of Dewey's view. Communal inquiry and discussion were central to his vision of growth.

And it isn't just a chore. Dewey celebrated the educative and enriching effects of open-minded and sympathetic democratic dialogue (e.g. 1916, MW 9:8–9; 1939, LW 14:228). *Democracy and Education* argues that personal growth involves willingness to engage with alien points of view (1916, MW 9:182). How does democratic dialogue help us grow? Dewey offers further details. It forces us to reflect imaginatively on our experience, to give it shape, to extract its net meaning, to find unanticipated points of contact with other human beings (1916, MW 9:8–9). The communication occurring in vitally shared social life allows all of us to join in the difficult task of articulating the purposes and meanings of our experience. Imaginative entry into another's perspective helps break the barriers between us. Sometimes it even creates the sense of "community of experience" (1934, LW 10:337–38). It forces us to reconstruct the image of the other, enabling us to see one another as if for the first time (1934, LW 10:59). It changes who we are:

> This educational process is based upon faith in human good sense and human good will as it manifests itself in the long run when communication is progressively liberated from bondage to prejudice and ignorance. It constitutes a firm and continuous reminder that the process of living together, when it is emancipated from oppressions and suppressions, becomes . . . a constant growth of that kind of understanding of our relations to one another that expels fear, suspicion and distrust. (1950, LW 17:86)

Like individuals, societies can also develop. On this level, too, "routine" habits may form barriers to human flourishing and development. Large-scale growth requires revising prevalent habits and improving social institutions to remove such barriers. Dewey often criticizes social arrangements and cultures based on the way in which they "hem in" human beings. For instance, unsatisfactory industrial arrangements relegate many workers to highly unfulfilling jobs. Racial and gender prejudice confine and oppress human beings (1922, MW 13:244). Social growth involves identifying such problems and solving them.[21] And this requires having a wider democratic conversation.[22] Citizens should be educated to take part in it.

With all his talk of problem-solving, it might seem that Dewey's perspective on learning was narrowly "utilitarian." It wasn't: Dewey opposed making rigid distinctions between the fine and the useful. Learning to see the beauty of line and color in modern painting is just as much an instance of growth as is figuring out what to do when we face a moral dilemma. Growth can occur in a wide range of settings. Coming to terms with an opposing point of view in a debate. Finding fresh means of communicating across the barriers that divide us. Engaging, imaginatively and sympathetically, with the lives of others. Making an effort to be conscious of the beauty of our everyday lives. All these experiences involve personal growth.

Dewey advocated facilitating "genuine development of individuality for the mass of individuals" (1934, LW 9:180). But this wasn't supposed to be a selfish, short-sighted, narrowly "individualistic" project. For Dewey believed that individuals can grow by taking part in larger human development—the creation and improvement of a thriving democratic culture that involves "mutual consultation and discussion" (1934, LW 9:180).

Fostering this was the real aim of Dewey's much-celebrated and much-misunderstood project in *Democracy and Education*. His most famous book isn't just about making sure that future citizens know their "civics." Nor is it just about introducing "progressive" classroom practices for their own sake. In place of the Simple Platonist's static, perfectionist utopia, it proposes facilitating the gradual co-development of personality and social life.

A thought-provoking goal. How exactly would taking part in shaping democratic life help citizens grow? Along what specific lines would the envisaged co-development of democratic societies and "democratic individuals" (1939, LW 14:92) occur? Only once we've grasped Dewey's answers can we truly say we've understood his vision of democratic education. His dialogue with Rousseau offers a helpful entry point into his complex vision of the co-development of democratic individuals and cultures.

§2.4. SUFFICIENT UNTO OURSELVES

The title of Rousseau's *Reveries of the Solitary Walker* speaks for itself. The book revels in solitude. It offers us a striking portrait of a socially disconnected self:

> These hours of *solitude* and meditation are the only ones in the day during which *I am fully myself* and for myself, without diversion, without obstacle, and during which I can truly claim to be *what nature willed.*

> Such is the state in which I often found myself during my solitary reveries on St. Peter's island, either lying in my boat as I let it drift with the water or seated on the banks of the tossing lake; or elsewhere, at the edge of a beautiful river or of a brook murmuring over pebbles. What do we enjoy in such a situation? Nothing external to ourselves, nothing if not ourselves and our own existence. As long as this state lasts, *we are sufficient unto ourselves, like God.*[23]

In the *Reveries*, being "fully oneself" involves shedding the many layers of inauthenticity that disfigure one's "original constitution."[24] Withdrawing from society, not social immersion, is what is needed. Dissimulation, convention, dependence on others—all this distorts the heart's "original inclinations," muddying the waters so much that our "true nature" can no longer be discerned.[25] From this standpoint Dewey's insistence on the importance of social immersion for the development of personality appears wrong-headed. Cultivating individuality, it might seem, has nothing to do with taking part in a thriving democratic culture. Dreaming alone on the banks of St. Peter's Island is required. Even *Emile*, a book that seeks to balance independence and fraternity, gestures at the delights of being alone: "Wherever there are men, I am in the home of my brothers; *wherever there are no men, I am in my own home*" (472, my emphasis).

Dewey was a serious reader of Rousseau, whose insights "repay careful study" (1916, MW 9:119). The American pragmatist read Rousseau as an ardent social critic who employed the rhetoric of nature to pave way for "social progress" (1916, MW 9:97). Of the movement to which Rousseau (on Dewey's view) belonged, he wrote: "In reality its chief interest was in progress and in social progress" (1916, MW 9:97). To focus merely on the critique of Rousseau's nonsocial conception of the self is to "convey only an inadequate ideal of the true significance of the movement" (1916, MW 9:97), for "the seeming antisocial philosophy was a somewhat transparent mask for an impetus toward a wider and freer society" (1916, MW 9:97–98). In addition to recognizing the critical force of Rousseau's conception of the "natural" self, Dewey also acknowledged that Rousseau was seeking a better society than the one that existed in his time: "We must not forget that Rousseau had the idea of a radically different sort of society, *a fraternal society* whose end should be identical with the good of all its members, which he thought to be as much better than existing states as these are worse than the state of nature" (1916, MW 9:125n2, my emphasis).

Needless to say, Dewey was sympathetic to the project. True, defective social institutions may constrain personal development. The two philosophers of education agreed on this essential point. Dewey embraced the spirit, but not the conclusions, of Rousseau's vision:

> *The doctrine of following nature . . . meant a rebellion against existing social institutions, customs, and ideals. . . .* It is upon this conception of *the artificial and harmful character of organized social life as it now exists* that he Rousseau rested the notion that nature not merely furnishes prime forces which initial growth but also its plan and goal. That evil institutions work almost automatically to give a wrong education which the most careful schooling cannot offset is true enough; *but the conclusion is not to educate apart from the social environment,* but to provide an environment in which native powers will be put to better uses. (1916, MW 9:124–25, my emphases)

It is hard not to be reminded of Rousseau when reading *Democracy and Education*'s lucid critique of the confining drudgery of formal schooling in early twentieth-century America. Dewey's most famous book shares in the spirit of Rousseau's project—its "impassioned devotion to emancipation of life from external restrictions" (1916, MW 9:98). But it rejects the Romantic notion that the "native endowment is . . . nonsocial or . . . antisocial" (1916, MW 9:97). The answer isn't to strip away all social influences to reveal a hidden "original constitution" in all its purity and perfection. It is to improve community life to allow richer development of personality.[26] *Democracy and Education* seeks to give schoolchildren a thriving social environment "in which native powers will be put to better uses" (1916, MW 9:124–25).

Dewey wasn't just a careful reader of Rousseau; he was also a serious student of Hegel. Eventually, he abandoned the Hegelianism of his early youth (see 1930, LW 5:153). But he continued emphasizing the social aspects of the self's formation. Hegel "destroyed completely . . . the psychology that regarded 'mind' as a ready-made possession of a naked individual by showing the significance of 'objective mind'—language, government, art, religion—in the formation of individual minds" (1916, MW 9:64). *Democracy and Education* bears traces of this influence:[27] "Through social intercourse, through sharing in activities embodying beliefs, he [the individual] gradually acquires a mind of his own. The conception of mind as a purely isolated possession of the self is at the very antipodes of the truth" (1916, MW 9:304, see also 1925, LW 1:187–88).

We will never be "sufficient unto ourselves, like God."[28] There might be transient moments—Rousseau's reveries on the banks of St. Peter's Island among them—when it might seem *as if* we were. But a proper understanding of how we become who we are reveals that the idea of an originally given, perfectly self-sufficient personality rests on an illusion.

Recognizing that social influences are essential to personal growth isn't the same as embracing all of them uncritically. We shouldn't just acquiesce in whatever social conditions we inhabit, a point on which Dewey criticized Hegel (1916, MW 9:65). Dewey was one of the greatest apologists for educating autonomous, creative individuals "who free their minds from the standards of the order which obtains" (1925, LW 1:169). When *Democracy and Education* argues "for the diversity of individual talent and for the need of free development of individuality in all its variety" (1916, MW 9:97), it echoes some of Rousseau's best insights.

What about the aesthetic richness of Rousseau's experience on St. Peter's Island? Was Dewey insensitive to the finer longings captured in the poetic passages cited earlier? I think not. Although a full account of this will have to wait until the next chapter, it is worth noting that Dewey shared in the Romantic aspiration to enhance the richness and the beauty of our lived experience. He dreamt of a time when "the hardness and crudeness of contemporary life will be bathed in the light that never was on land or sea" (1920, MW 12:200–201). "The light that never was on land or sea" is, after all, a reference to Wordsworth's *Elegiac Stanzas.*

As Dewey saw it, sharing in the spirit of the Romantic project doesn't necessarily mean literally going back to "nature," "withdrawing from the hub of society."[29] The flourishing and richness of experience that the Romantics sought doesn't lie in uncovering some "original" human essence, lost in a distant past.[30] The answer to our problems lies in gradual human development. That is the Deweyan alternative. Not rejecting civilization, but continually improving the way we live to remove the sources of confinement and suffering that make the Romantic rhetoric so enticing.

§2.5. CULTIVATING INDIVIDUALITY

Dewey's dialogue with Rousseau contains a provocative line of thought. When it comes to cultivating individuality, the answer isn't "withdrawing from the hub of society."[31] It is social immersion, but only of a certain kind. Oppressive, conformist, authoritarian cultures may stifle the growth of individuality. Dewey recognized this. That is part of the reason why Dewey defended democracy. In an early essay, "The Ethics of Democracy" (1888, EW 1:244), Dewey explained his preference for democracy over the Platonic Republic. He recognized the charm of the latter but criticized it for slotting individuals into predefined positions, without giving them the chance for self-determination. By contrast, democracy gives individuals a chance to develop autonomy, creativity, and initiative: "it is also true (and this is the truth omitted by aristocracy, emphasized by democracy) that he [the individual] must find this place in society and assume this work in the main for himself. . . . This fulfilling of function in devotion to the interests of the social organism, is not to be put into a man from without. It must begin in the man himself. . . . Personal responsibility, individual initiation, these are the notes of democracy" (1888, EW 1:244). That is also why he bothered criticizing schools in early twentieth-century America. Their excessively authoritative teaching methods smothered the nascent individual, suppressing creativity, initiative, and autonomy (1916, MW 9:159–60).

The fundamental dichotomy isn't between living alone and living with others. It is between confining, oppressive social interactions and those that furnish opportunities for creativity, initiative, criticism, for the expression of one's "irreducible uniqueness" (1925, LW 1:187) within the social matrix. In other words, the answer lies in the *quality* of social interactions—not their absence. Communities that encourage the cultivation of individuality can be built. Dewey hoped that schools would become such communities. And so would democracies.

Of course, much more still has to be said to flesh out this view. Dewey never gave us all the details. But what he told us is enough to reconstruct the outlines of his unorthodox position.

Experience and Nature emphasizes the dialogue between self and society whereby a growing person acquires an "individualized mind" (1925, LW 1:188). Dewey developed his view against the backdrop of a historical narrative about the "ancients" and the "Romantics." As he saw it, the ancients failed to recognize the distinctive value of individuality. Complete conformity of the individual to the group or family was required. Social criticism was illegitimate (1925, LW 1:164).

Even artists were expected not to question preestablished patterns (1925, LW 1:166). A revolution occurred when the creative force of individuality was explicitly embraced. The Romantics realized that social progress can occur when creative individuals "who free their minds from the standards of the order which obtains" make an effort to criticize and improve society (1925, LW 1:169). Dewey wanted to preserve the critical force of the Romantic movement. But he didn't want to adopt their problematic notion of an "original," presocial self.[32]

Charging the ancients with ignoring individuality may have been uncharitable on Dewey's part. After all, in Plato's *Symposium*, Socrates is praised for being "unique; he is like no one else. . . . This is by far the most amazing thing about him. . . . There is a parallel for everyone—everyone else, that is."[33] The story told in *Experience and Nature* may not be historically accurate, but it helps clarify Dewey's own position.

The key difficulty in understanding his alternative lies in making sense of what he called an individual's "irreducible uniqueness" (1925, LW 1:187). It cannot reside in some completely formed, originally given, presocial self. Dewey's answer is elusive. We never receive a clear definition. I take "irreducible uniqueness" to be a collection of "native tendencies," expressed and developed in interactions between organism and environment.

Individuality emerges when we interact with and reshape our material and social environment—in a way that reflects our unique tendencies that are, in a sense that Dewey never explained, prior to these activities (1925, LW 1:168). But if there are no original, presocial selves, who exactly are the "we" that interact with and are acted on by the environment? Perhaps Dewey thought that persons develop from biological organisms.[34] They become genuine "individuals" only when they engage in a creative remaking of the world in a way that expresses their "native tendencies" (1916, MW 9:180). This means that individuality isn't given to us at the get-go. We can't find out "who we are" by recovering some lost "original" self. Individuality "is not something complete in itself, like a closet in a house or a secret drawer in a desk, filled with treasures that are waiting to be bestowed on the world. . . . It develops into shape and form only through interaction with actual conditions." Individual manner is "formed in the very process of creation of other things" (1930, LW 5:122–23).

Dewey wasn't just a simple-minded apologist for community as such. He recognized that we can find ourselves "at odds with our . . . surroundings." This can become a source of "bitter loneliness." Perhaps rather optimistically, he didn't think this sort of solitude is an essential part of the human condition. We aren't locked in a prison of "a vast and somnambulic egotism." We can reshape the world. We can change the way we live together. We can break through the barriers that divide us: "In science and in art, especially in the art of intercourse, real solutions occur. Private bias manages in them to manifest itself in innovations and deviations, which reshape the world of objects and institutions, and which eventually facilitate communication and understanding" (1925, LW 1:187–88).

Sometimes we are able to overcome problems of adjustment with the social environment. This happens when draw on our irreducible uniqueness to produce valuable, communicable results. This is precisely how genuine individuality emerges, on his view. When the individual actively sets out to reshape the environment in response to problems, she can develop "mind as individualized, initiating, adventuring, experimenting, dissolving" (1925, LW 1:188). Dewey's reference to "the art of intercourse" signals just how important social interactions are to this sort of growth. The reshaping of conditions also requires breaking away from established habits:

> I say individual minds, not just individuals with minds. The difference between the two ideas is radical. . . . the whole history of science, art and morals proves that the mind that appears in individuals is not as such individual mind. The former is in itself a system of belief, recognitions, and ignorances, of acceptances and rejections, of expectancies and appraisals of meanings which have been instituted under the influence of custom and tradition. (1925, LW 1:169–70)

Dewey's works provide us with an alternative to the "Romantic" view. When it comes to cultivating individuality, what is needed is enhancing the quality of our engagement with the social environment—not its absence. Recovering a mythical "original self" isn't required. Nor is seeking the sparsely populated pastoral utopia depicted in *Emile*. Although the individual possesses some biological tendencies to which her originality might ultimately be traced, fully developed originality is an achievement. Creative individuality, capable of breaking through established norms and customs, is developed in a constructive dialogue with the social environment. This requires developing the ability "to break away from current and established classifications and interpretations of the world" (1925, LW 1:170). *Experience and Nature* argues in favor of learning to take active control of one's environment. It celebrates openness, flexibility, and the ability to let go of the security and ease afforded to the organism by its current adjustments to the environment (1925, LW 1:189). Learning to communicate, cooperate, and connect with others is also crucial. Hence the importance of educating human beings to take part in dialogue; hence Dewey's insistence that mediocrity shouldn't be thought of as an ineradicable feature of the "mass" (e.g., 1922, MW 13:289–94).[35]

"A vast and somnambulic egotism" (1925, LW 1:187–88)—that is how Dewey characterized the Romantic movement. That is probably how he would have characterized Rousseau's reveries on St. Peter's Island. Rousseau might have replied that Dewey never fully addressed his fundamental concern: that social connectedness has a darker side. It can foster passions that distort our lives: vanity, competitiveness, deceitfulness, the desire to manipulate, oppress, and dominate others.[36] (Which is why Rousseau celebrated escaping the influences of society, why he reveled in the peace of solitude.) Of course, Dewey recommended educating human beings for "common understanding . . . mutual sympathy and goodwill among all peoples and races" (1934, LW 9:203–4). But he never said specifically how he would deal with the existence of the darker passions that so worried Rousseau.

Emile sees these passions as the result of our mutual dependence. Only independence, on Rousseau's view, can help forestall the emergence of vanity, domination, competitiveness, the "comparative" urge. That is why the book suggests taking the child away from society before the dark passions take root. Dewey recommends the opposite: social immersion. But how would the "miniature communities" (1916, MW 9:370) he envisaged steer clear of the dangers identified by Rousseau? To be sure, fostering cooperation and sympathy in schools would be wonderful. But Dewey never fully explored the *barriers* that teachers might face when they try to do this. Rousseau did. He saw vanity as the greatest barrier to sympathy. He saw social life (at least as it existed in bourgeois France) as a fertile ground for vanity. Dewey was probably right that cultivating individuality requires social immersion. But he should have probed the darker sides of social connectedness in more depth.

§2.6. CITIZENS AND
PHILOSOPHER-KINGS

"Until philosophers rule as kings . . . cities will have no rest from evils . . . nor, I think, will the human race."[37] Whether offered in seriousness or in jest, the remark remains as provocative today as it was in Plato's time. Dewey spent much of his long career debating it. His vast oeuvre puts forward different reasons to resist the Simple Platonist position. The vision is "not equal to reality; it is not equal to the actual forces animating men as they work in history . . . the practical consequence of giving the few wise and good power is that they cease to remain wise and good" (1888, EW 1:242). Philosopher-kings don't know enough about the life and the needs of the rest of us (1888, EW 1:242; 1927, LW 2:364). Nor should we trust them to tell us what the "end" of existence is (1916, MW 9:94–95). No single sage has access to "the good, as something itself attained and formulated in philosophy" (1925, LW 1:305). Everyone should have a chance to get involved in figuring out how we should live.

Another reason emerges from the discussion in §2.5. Cultivating genuine individuality requires taking an active part in determining the social conditions under which you live, in dialogue with other citizens. Merely being slotted into a predetermined position isn't enough (1888, EW 1:242). A thriving liberal democratic culture would enrich our characters as we engage in the demanding project of figuring out how we should live together. That is partly why Dewey cautioned against the false appeal of any but "liberal democratic means" to achieve "security for individuals and opportunity for their development as personalities" (1937, LW 11:298). Dictatorships may claim these ends, too. But they forget that the development of genuine personality is bound up with taking part in the remaking of the social matrix you inhabit—in free, open-minded, sympathetic dialogue and inquiry with others. Unlike the Simple Platonist, "democracy . . . holds . . . that personality cannot be procured for any one, however degraded and feeble, by any one else, however wise and strong" (1888, EW 1:244).

In 1939, Dewey took the trouble to clarify this view. He was worried that some of his earlier statements—that "what the individual actually *is* in his life-experience depends upon the nature and the movement of associated life"—were misleading. "The rise of dictatorships and . . . decline of democracy" (1939, LW 14:91) prompted him to shift emphasis:

> In re-thinking the issue in the light of the rise of totalitarian states, *I am led to emphasize the idea that only the voluntary initiative and voluntary cooperation of individuals can produce social institutions that will protect the liberties necessary for achieving development of genuine individuality.*
>
> This change in emphasis does not in any way minimize the belief that the ability of individuals to develop genuine individuality is intimately connected with the social conditions under which they associate with one other. *But it attaches fundamental importance to the activities of individuals in determining the social conditions under which they live.* (1939, LW 14:92, my emphases)

Although Dewey writes as if this were a serious shift, his earlier writings already contain the strand of thought offered here. *Democracy and Education* is informed by Dewey's sense of the "fundamental importance of . . . the activities of individuals in determining the social conditions under which they live" (1939, LW 14:92). This is made particularly clear in the passages where Dewey resists the anti-individualism of Hegel's thought:

Against institutions as they are, individuals have no spiritual rights; *personal development,* and nurture, *consist in obedient assimilation of the spirit of existing institutions.* Conformity, not transformation, is the essence of education. Institutions change as history shows; but their change, the rise and fall of states, is the work of the "world-spirit." *Individuals,* save the great "heroes" who are the chosen organs of the world-spirit, *have no share or lot in it.* (1916, MW 9:64, my emphases)

Democratic citizenship isn't about conformity to a preset pattern. We shouldn't simply fit into the democratic way of life as it exists. We should take part in making it better (1916, MW 9:84–85). And this will help us grow. The view that "personal development . . . consists in obedient assimilation of the spirit of existing institutions" (1916, MW 9:64) is the antithesis of Dewey's position. *Democracy and Education* ends with a plea for forming "a character which . . . is interested in the continuous readjustment . . . essential to growth" (1916, MW 9:370). Schooling should prepare democratic citizens to take an active part in the reshaping of personal and social habits in response to problems, in sympathetic dialogue with others. This, of course, aligns with the vision of growth outlined earlier in §2.3.

Recall the contrast with Simple Platonism offered in chapter 1. The Simple Platonist seeks to use schooling to institute a fixed, ideal way of life based on a predetermined pattern accessible to the wise few (1916, MW 9:94–95). By contrast, *Democracy and Education* seeks to facilitate "growth" (1916, MW 9:56)—the continual revision of our individual and collective habits. The goal of Deweyan education isn't utopian stasis. It is instead the creation of an evolving community—one that develops itself by constantly solving the new problems it faces in order to reduce human suffering and liberate human capacities, and one that "endeavors to shape the experiences of the young so that instead of reproducing current habits, better habits shall be formed, and thus the future adult society be an improvement on their own." Dewey didn't look to philosopher-kings to take charge of human development. He wanted democratic citizens to do the work. The community he envisaged develops in a direction set by its members, who have attained the capacity to take part in defining and seeking the good life together.[38]

The *Republic* charges democracies with "breeding anarchy."[39] Its ideal community is a static utopia, designed to guard against democratic chaos. The Deweyan alternative to Simple Platonism isn't rudderless vacillation and anarchy. It is a modern conception of democracy as a way of life that enables gradual human development. The pragmatic meliorist seeks a liberal way to promote human flourishing—by engaging all human beings in the project of improving life. This, of course, requires an ambitious program of education to foster growth-enabling skills.

§2.7. CITIZEN EDUCATION BEYOND "CIVICS"

Now we have a fresh perspective on *Democracy and Education*. Deweyan democratic schooling aims to facilitate a creative, constructive dialogue between the self and society. He hoped that this would simultaneously enrich both democratic individuals and democratic culture. A thriving democratic community would give us opportunities to reshape the way we live together (in consultation with others).[40] And it would develop our personalities in the process. Schooling should prepare us for this educative give-and-take.

All this, of course, connects to Dewey's central idea of democracy as a dynamic, evolving culture:[41] "Democracy is a moving thing. . . . Its possibilities are far from exhausted." Democracy isn't something ready-made. It isn't fully exemplified in the existing institutions. It demands constant elaboration. We must continually search for better means to realize it (1927, LW 2:325). Democracy is "creative" (1939, LW 14:225; 1927, LW 2:256–57; 1937, LW 11:182).[42] It "must be continually explored afresh" (LW 11:182). Citizen education must form "democratic individuals" who will contribute to creating and elaborating the democratic way of life in dialogue with each other (1939, LW 14:226). This sort of mutual engagement is educative in the "largest sense" (1930, LW 5:289).

This takes us far from the "thin" view of democratic education that's limited to teaching "civics." Schooling should promote the intellectual and affective habits citizens need to engage in this growth-enabling dialogue. What habits? Dewey doesn't give an exhaustive picture. He offers us a starting point for reflection (see 1933, LW 9:152). *Democracy and Education* echoes *Experience and Nature* when it emphasizes the value of open-mindedness, responsibility in considering the consequences of one's actions and habits (1916, MW 9:366–267); sympathy, communicative and cooperative skills (1916, MW 9:127); initiative in reshaping world and self; willingness to risk giving up the security of established habits.[43] *Human Nature and Conduct* emphasizes the value of creativity, considering a wide range of possibilities, entering imaginatively into other points of view (1922, MW 14:139).[44] When widely shared, such growth-enabling habits can set individuals and communities on a path to further development. *Democracy and Education* charges the formal schooling of its time with instilling habits of detachment, apathy, narrow-mindedness, and passive obedience instead of fostering habits that enable growth.

It should be clear by now that Deweyan growth doesn't occur in solitude. Dialogue is central to Deweyan democracy. It isn't a coincidence that communication is crucial to his conception of how the individual develops, too. The two strands of thought are brought together in his works. One of his main concerns was improving communication across interpersonal and intergroup divides. He was worried about the hatreds, misunderstandings, and prejudices that estrange us from one another (1916, MW 9:182, 343; 1934, LW 9:203–4). What attitudes and habits might help us break through the barriers between us? "Creative Democracy" addresses the question. It emphasizes the importance of tolerance, trust, sympathy, and the habit of resolving conflicts through dialogue rather than force (1939, LW 14:228). Those with whom we disagree should be seen as those from whom we might learn. The democratic way of life requires that we adopt a certain way of seeing one another—as engaged in a joint enterprise of working out how we should live together. This attitude involves flexibility and open-mindedness. Being able to respect other points of view is also important. Perhaps this requires some humility.[45]

This facet of Dewey's conception of the democratic way of life is expressed in his unequivocal condemnation of racial (1922, MW 13:242–43) and gender prejudice (e.g., 1922, MW 13:248).[46] His plea for a reconstruction of habits connects to his suggestion that prejudices can be understood as defective, sometimes unconscious, habits of seeing the other (1922, MW 13:244). Prejudices and stereotypes confine human beings and impoverish human experience. Deweyan democracy seeks a community in which they would be overcome. The moral meaning of democracy is "to set free and to develop the capacities of human

individuals without respect to race, sex, class or economic status" (1920, MW 12:186). Schooling should prepare us to take
part in the creation of a community that exemplifies this vision.

At first sight, Dewey's dictum that "the object and reward of
learning is continued capacity for growth" (1916, MW 9:105)
sounds like a fuzzy cliche. But it contains a meliorist insight.
We shouldn't expect schools to create "omnicompetent" citizens.[47] Nor should we be discouraged when we realize that this
is impossible. Dewey's alternative envisages preparing citizens
for a lifelong educative project of mutual engagement and creative remaking of the way they live together. They will continue
growing as they take part in a thriving democratic way of life.
Deweyan democratic education doesn't aim at the impossible
ideal of cultivating citizens who are experts in every field.
Instead, it focuses on promoting the intellectual and affective
habits they need to develop themselves and their communities.

The vision sounds attractive. But can it be realized? Cultivating character is challenging. A skeptic might object that
formal instruction isn't going to further the desired skills.
Dewey recognized the worry. He cautioned that "merely adding on a special course for direct instruction in good behavior"
isn't likely to be effective. His vision was far more ambitious.
The school ought to be "organized as a community in which
pupils share," one that "would give practice in the give and take
of social life, practice in methods of cooperation, and would
require assumption of definite responsibilities" (1943, LW 9:192).
In other words, students can develop growth-enabling habits by
practicing them in "miniature communities" (1916, MW 9:370)
that embody the democratic ethos. Much like the wider democratic society, those communities should be diverse and inclusive. *Democracy and Education* argues that schools should cut
across social divides. "The School as Social Centre" takes

inspiration from the Hull House settlement when it echoes this position:[48]

> There is mixing people up with each other; bringing them together under wholesome influences, and under conditions which will promote their getting acquainted with the best side of each other. . . . It is not merely a place where ideas and beliefs may be exchanged, not merely in the arena of formal discussion . . . but in ways where ideas are incarnated in human form and clothed with the winning grace of personal life. (1902, MW 2:90–91)

"The winning grace of personal life," Dewey knew full well, can be a lot more powerful than abstract admonitions. To enhance character education, we should improve the form of social life present in the school environment. Dewey focused on the values the school actually exemplifies. On the habits it promotes by virtue of how it is organized. On who gets to be part of it. On the kinds of interactions it encourages. He argued that formal educational settings should help us overcome the barriers that divide us. They should do this, at least in part, by virtue of their makeup and organization. Overcoming these divides in formal educational settings can help pave way for making gradual improvements in our wider democratic culture: in schools "we may produce a projection in the type of society we should like to realize, and by forming minds in accord with it gradually modify the larger and more recalcitrant features of adult society" (1916, MW 9:326). Democratic schooling should liberate human capacities "without respect to race, sex, class or economic status" (1902, MW 12:186). And it should help pupils learn to engage in constructive dialogue (1902, MW 2:85).

We should also take a fresh look at our teaching methods. *Democracy and Education* aims to awaken creativity, initiative, and responsibility. It seeks to spark spontaneous engagement by opening up room for individual contributions, by involving students in congenial projects. This, of course, is the antithesis of "rote learning." We can now clearly see why Dewey advocated his well-known "progressive" teaching techniques. He wanted to facilitate a constructive, creative dialogue between the self and the social matrix (§2.5–6). In 1934 Dewey reflected on the influence of propaganda on the population. He argued that schooling might help remedy the situation by fostering the habits of inquiry, curiosity and "intelligent skepticism:"

> Many young people leave school with the attitude of wanting and expecting to be *told*, rather than with the attitude of realizing that they must look into things, must inquire and examine. There is complaint, and rightly, that the population is too amenable, on the whole, to the influence of propaganda. But why is it? Why are so many people so ready to swallow what is persistently told them, or told them with an air of authority? . . . It is because they have acquired the habit of listening and of accepting, instead of that of inquiry, and, if you please, of intelligent skepticism. (1934, LW 9:159)

Are our schools successful in preparing democratic citizens? The question cannot be answered by looking at standardized scores. It cannot be answered by looking at how well students "assimilate" preset subject matter in specific domains, be it "civics" or STEM. Dewey challenges us to take a hard look at each school's makeup, organization, and teaching techniques. What intellectual and affective habits do they actually form? In an age when standardized scores and subject "coverage" reign supreme in school assessments, Dewey reminds us that the task of schooling isn't just intellectual. It is also social and moral.

This doesn't mean, of course, that Dewey offered us the whole answer:

> In a world changing as rapidly as ours, in a democracy with so short a history to draw on for choice of the best ways to succeed, expression of differences of opinions by different kinds of schools is a wholesome sign. In developing anything new, it is a good plan to have different methods working side by side, to experiment, to compare. . . . Progressive education has not one formula, it is not a fixed and finished thing. (1933, LW 9:152)

He shouldn't be read as though he discovered the Platonic form of democratic education. There's still plenty of room for debate and experimentation. More important than the worth of his specific proposals is the larger project he placed at the center of political philosophy. Those who work on democratic education should be seen as making important contributions to an ongoing conversation that is essential for our discipline—and for our times.[49]

§2.8. THE RANGE AND CHALLENGE OF THE PROJECT

Dewey's vision of democratic education already looks ambitious. It becomes even more so when we add another piece of the puzzle. Preparing citizens to pursue fulfilling callings that contribute to society is a neglected yet crucial area of democratic education: "An occupation is the only thing which balances the distinctive capacity of an individual with his social service. To find out what one is fitted to do and to secure an opportunity to do it is the key to happiness. Nothing is more tragic than failure to discover one's true business in life, or to find that one has drifted or been forced by circumstance into an uncongenial calling" (1916, MW 9:318).[50]

He agreed with Plato that a society gets the best from individuals when they do what is suited to them; education must disclose their talents. But he rejected the idea of slotting individuals into fixed classes (1916, MW 9:94). Already in his earliest writings, Dewey insisted on the importance of the individual's finding her vocation for herself (1888, EW 1:244). By respecting individual diversity and the breadth of the human potential for development, education may facilitate personal growth and enhance community life. Dewey disagreed with the Platonic view that philosophers should be responsible for finding out the ends of existence and outlining the optimal organization of community (1916, MW 9:95). He also resisted the "Romantic" overemphasis on detaching the individual from the social matrix. A genuine democracy would open up space for diversity and creativity, for varied and open-ended personal growth in the sphere of work. By exercising growth-enabling habits in congenial work projects, individuals would contribute to human development on a larger scale. Vocational education should help human beings find suitable callings and keep growing in them.

This sort of education shouldn't just be a luxury for the few. Dewey was worried about the "vast amount of unutilized talent" in contemporary societies (1902, MW 2:92). He was also concerned that the increasing specialization and complexity of modern life often makes it difficult for individuals to appreciate the social meaning of their work. Being unable to make—or grasp—one's contribution to society can be alienating.[51] It can result in social fragmentation that undermines democracy. By contrast, recognizing the social bearings of one's work can help one feel like a "vital part of the whole" (1902, MW 2:88).

Democratic education should remedy the situation (1902, MW 2:89). It should open up human potential. It should help individuals find a way to make a meaningful contribution to their community. And it should help them appreciate the social utility of their work (e.g. 1902, MW 2:89; 1916, MW 9:324; 1937, LW 11:188). "The Challenge of Democracy to Education" echoes these ideas: "It [vocational education] may prepare them quite effectively on the technical side and yet leave graduates with very little understanding of the place of those industries or professions in the social life of the present, and of what these vocations and professions may do to keep democracy a living, growing thing" (1937, LW 11:188).

Dewey recognized another looming problem: as society develops, many occupations become obsolete. Those who don't get a chance to adapt may feel alienated, left behind by the rest of society. This can also undermine democracy. We should provide individuals with lifelong educational opportunities designed to help them adapt to changing conditions (1902, MW 2:89). This, too, is part of democratic education.

What exactly was Dewey's conception of "social utility"? Are students to choose only callings that contribute to the status quo at the expense of pursuits that might challenge it? Dewey believed that originality and nonconformism are important for communal development. We shouldn't conceive social efficiency too narrowly: "It covers all that makes one's own experience more worthwhile to others, and all that enables one to participate more richly in the worthwhile experiences of others" (1916, MW 9:127). Conscientious objectors and "social innovators" are socially valuable—and so are those who pursue what might at first sight appear to be "luxurious callings:" science and art (1922, MW 13:297). Dewey insisted on the importance of contributing to one's community in a vocational setting. But he combined this with a liberal approach that gives individuals the final say in defining their "social service": "Social efficiency, even social service, are hard and metallic things when severed from an active acknowledgment of the diversity of goods which life may afford to different persons, and from faith in the social utility of encouraging every individual to make his own choice intelligent" (1916, MW 9:127).

Helping individuals find fulfilling vocations will enhance their contributions to society. But this isn't the only reason why we should enrich vocational training. Another reason is fulfilling democracy's moral ideal—"to set free and to develop the capacities of human individuals without respect to race, sex, class or economic status." Too many human beings are confined to unfulfilling, uncongenial jobs. Worse still, vocational training may end up slotting them into such jobs based on their "race, sex, class or economic status" (1920, MW 12:186). Dewey's critique of the injustice of this system resonates with W. E. B. Du Bois's concerns. The two philosophers can be seen as allies in their impassioned criticisms of the oppressive and confining effects of the vocational training of their time. Du Bois provides a particularly helpful perspective that illuminates the racial injustice inherent in that system:

> Is not life more than meat, and the body more than raiment? And men ask this to-day all the more eagerly because of sinister signs in recent educational movements. The tendency is here, born of slavery and quickened to renewed life by the crazy imperialism of the day, to regard human beings as among the material resources of a land to be trained with an eye single to future dividends. Race-prejudices, which keep brown and black men in their "places," we are coming to regard as useful allies with such a theory, no matter how much they may dull the ambition and sicken

the hearts of struggling human beings. And above all, we daily hear that an education that encourages aspiration, that sets the loftiest of ideals and seeks as an end culture and character rather than bread-winning, is the privilege of white men and the danger and delusion of black.[52]

At its best, the American philosophical tradition has included voices—Du Bois's and Dewey's prominent among them—that conceived of American democracy not just as the "least bad" set of governmental institutions, but as a vast, demanding project aimed at creating a growth-enabling culture for all human beings, irrespective of their race, sex, class, or economic status.[53]

Of course, much more can and should be said about vocational education. In this brief overview, my aim is only to indicate its importance to Dewey's project. Once that is fully appreciated, we go beyond the narrow view focused on preparing citizens to vote.

Adding this piece of the puzzle helps us see the picture whole. Now we are in a position to answer the question posed earlier (§2.3). Along what lines would the envisaged co-development between the "democratic individual" and democratic community occur? Dewey's answer was expansive. The self and society will grow as individuals engage in remaking their habits in the interest of enhancing human flourishing. They can do this by changing the way they treat each other in everyday life. By engaging in a wider democratic dialogue that offers further opportunities for growth as it shapes all those who take part in it. By pursuing their callings. Democratic education should foster all these lines of co-development:

> Democracy demands a more thoroughgoing education than the education of officials, administrators and directors of industry.

Because this fundamental general education is at once so necessary and so difficult of achievement, the enterprise of democracy is so challenging. To sidetrack it to the task of enlightenment of administrators and executives is to miss something of *its range and its challenge*. (1922, MW 13:344, my emphasis)

§2.9. THEORIST OF DEMOCRATIC EDUCATION

The scope of theorizing democratic education has been enlarged. It involves investigating the co-development of personality and social life. As theorist of democratic education, Dewey no longer looks like a superficial thinker. Few issues are more profound.

Talk of Deweyan democratic education conjures up worn cliches: participatory classrooms, compulsory group work, teachers stripped of all habitual authority. It's time to change this shallow and unfaithful portrait; Dewey explicitly distanced himself from "progressivism" in education simplistically understood as a movement that entirely rejects teacher authority, and, for that matter, from all "isms" (see 1938, LW 13:4). These cliches have obscured much greater insights. Buried among discussions on the role of geography in school curricula are profound reflections on democracy, on how it can be nurtured—and on why we should bother.

Much of Dewey's fame rests on his vision of schooling in *Democracy and Education*. How can formal instruction cultivate good citizens? This is clearly the focus when he argues in favor of connecting high school subjects to current social problems (1916, MW 9:200). Or when he counsels enhancing the autonomy of future citizens by abandoning authoritative classroom practices in favor of congenial projects that involve creative experimentation (1916, MW 9:159–60). Or when he recommends that schools be made into "miniature communities" (1916, MW 9:370) that teach cooperative and communicative skills that future citizens will need. Understanding this part of the story has obvious contemporary relevance. Cultivating democratic character will help us strengthen the democratic way of life.

But this isn't all that Dewey has to offer us in these dark times. He also examines how democracy itself shapes us. For "democracy is an educative process" (1950, LW 17:86). Scattered throughout his vast oeuvre are numerous remarks about the formative effects of a flourishing democratic culture. We're told that "democracy . . . expels fear, suspicion and distrust" (1950, LW 17:86). Democratic dialogue can have transformative effects. Taking part in shaping democratic life can help us grow (1920, MW 12:199). These ideas, too, can help address the disenchantment of our times. They stand as a reminder of why we should cherish and elaborate the democratic ethos. Against all naysayers, Dewey tells us that the personalities developed in this process are rich and flourishing.

These strands of thought are connected. The point of formal schooling is to prepare us for lifelong growth in a thriving democratic society. Dewey's celebrated thoughts on "progressive" schooling cannot be fully understood in isolation from his vision of the overarching educative project to which the early period of formal instruction serves as a sort of prelude. Democratic schooling isn't just about preparing citizens to vote. The goal is far more substantial:

> The something for which a man must be good is capacity to live as a social member so that what he gets from living with others balances with what he contributes. What he gets and gives as a

human being . . . is not external possessions, but a widening and deepening of conscious life—a more intense, disciplined, and expanding realization of meanings. What he materially receives and gives is at most opportunities and means for *the evolution of conscious life*. . . . Discipline, culture, social efficiency, personal refinement, improvement of character are but phases of *the growth of capacity nobly to share in such a balanced experience*. And education is not a mere means to such a life. Education is such a life. (1916, MW 9:369–70, my emphases)

As theorist of democratic education, Dewey actually offers us two main lines of inquiry. One investigates the co-development of personalities and communities that happens in a flourishing democratic culture. Another seeks the sort of schooling that would facilitate this co-development. The two strands are connected by an overarching concern for growth. Large-scale social development can be facilitated through democratic schooling by creating citizens who will improve the way we live together. Personal growth is enhanced when individuals take part in this democratic project. These different facets of "democratic education" are explored in his works.

This neat picture might seem troubling. Isn't Dewey's emphasis on fostering the co-development of personality and social life utopian? Aren't there cases when the two are in tension?[54] I think the best way to read Dewey is as a meliorist.[55] We needn't follow him in seeking wholesale harmony. Instead, we should see him as having identified several potential lines along which the co-development of individual and society might be enhanced. This doesn't mean that we will ever be able to erase all tensions, creating a perfect virtuous circle between the growth of self and society. Dewey was overly optimistic about this. But we can certainly learn from his efforts to identify—and to enhance—potential synergies between the two goals. The meliorist version of the project actually aligns with Dewey's conception of human development better than does the utopian. Growth is a never-ending process of facing various problems and tensions. We cannot eradicate all of them forever, but we can still make improvements. Pragmatic meliorism provides us with a useful alternative to both utopianism and disenchantment.

Now we can see that Dewey wasn't just a simple-minded advocate of group work. His theory of democratic schooling is part and parcel of a penetrating inquiry that still demands our careful attention. Its central question, simply put, is this: how can education help us continually improve the way we live? Dewey tells us that the proper goal of democratic schooling is "the evolution of conscious life" (1916, MW 9:369–70). The phrase reveals the staggering scope of the proposed program. It isn't confined to teaching "civics." A vast picture of human development informs it. Having reconstructed it in §2.3, we can now grasp the significance of his neglected work.

What does this have to do with democracy? The commonplace conception of citizenship—limited to informed voting— has little to do with Dewey's expansive vision. "Change the image of what constitutes citizenship and you change the image of what is the purpose of the school" (1902, MW 2:83). So what constitutes citizenship, on his view? Taking part in the creation of an evolving culture that seeks to remove barriers to human flourishing through free consultation, open-minded inquiry, voluntary cooperation, creative experimentation, and sympathetic engagement with a wide range of human predicaments. Dewey's vision of democracy was unorthodox. It isn't just a system of government, handed to us ready-made, but an evolving culture that we should help develop. Its promise is vast: not merely electing our officials, but gradually pushing back the boundaries that "hem us in." Growing together.

A "thin" view of democracy sees it as the "least bad" set of institutions. Dewey offered us a competing "thick" conception. He saw it as an evolving culture that facilitates personal and social growth. We shouldn't just grudgingly tolerate its current failings. We are responsible for making it better. Democratic schooling should cultivate the skills we need to do this.

§2.10. DEMOCRACY UNDER THREAT

A fresh picture of the Deweyan "democratic individual" (1939, LW 14:92) can now be added to the hall of democratic personalities. She is nothing like the "lawless," rudderless, undisciplined dilettante criticized in the *Republic*.[56] She is a developing person. She grows in intelligence, creativity, and sympathy together with the community of which she is a part. She is able to revise her habits, to cooperate and communicate with others, to assess the social bearings of her own actions and habits—and of those of her community. This person grows as she participates in the "creation" of the democratic way of life. Dewey believed such growth isn't just open to members of a "small group" who "have tasted how sweet and blessed a possession philosophy is."[57] At least in principle, all of us can enjoy it.

Why bother reconstructing Dewey's vision of "democratic individuals?" It indicates the lines along which we can improve our schooling and our public life to strengthen the democratic ethos. But it also does more. It tells us why we should care. It stands as a reminder of democracy's best promise. Against all naysayers, Dewey tells us that a thriving democratic culture creates rich personalities and worthwhile lives. In dark times, it can inspire us to renew our commitment to democracy, showing us why we should try "to make the democratic way of life a deeper and wider reality than it has been" (1941, LW 14:264–65).

As we face democracy's troubles, we could do worse than turn to Dewey for a dose of democratic faith. Disillusionment is always enticing; it seems sophisticated, worldly-wise. When taken too far, the sentiment becomes an existential threat to democracy. It's always tempting to say: "Just give *us* absolute power and we'll set the world right." Dewey cautions against the false appeal of any but "liberal democratic means" to achieve our ends: "democracy means not only the ends which even dictatorships now assert are their ends, security for individuals and opportunity for their development as personalities. It signifies also primary emphasis upon the *means* by which these ends are to be fulfilled" (1937, LW 11:298). What are these means? They are, he tells us, "the voluntary activities of individuals in opposition to coercion; they are assent and consent in opposition to violence" (1937, LW 11:298). They are "consultation . . . conference . . . persuasion . . . discussion in the formation of public opinion" (1937, LW 11:227). Solving problems by free consultation and voluntary cooperation, not force.

All this might sound good, but what about democracy's failures? It's hard not to respond to them with disillusionment and skepticism. American pragmatism offers us an alternative. Learn to see democracy as an ethos for which we are responsible. Improve it gradually. Our efforts, it tells us, "carry the universe forward" (1925, LW 1:214).

Dewey tells us that totalitarianism succeeds, that democracy falls, when our democratic culture isn't strong enough. This happens when, in our public and private lives, we are animated not by a shared commitment to the democratic project, but by hatred, prejudice, and mistrust. A thriving democratic ethos is a safeguard against the decay and failure of our institutions. And it is also more. It is within that culture that many of democracy's highest hopes can be gradually realized. Democracy isn't just about occasional voting. It flourishes in how we treat each other.

What Walt Whitman said in *Democratic Vistas* might as well have been written by Dewey: "Did you, too, o friend, suppose democracy was only for elections, for politics, and for a party name? I say democracy is only of use there that it may pass on and *come to its flower and fruits in manners, in the highest forms of interaction* between men, and their beliefs—in religion, literature, colleges and schools—democracy in all public and private life, and in the army and navy."[58]

That is why in 1941 Dewey called on his young audience to make "creative effort" to realize democracy. We shouldn't take ourselves to be mere passive observers of world history, watching as it crushes our best hopes. Still, perhaps his audience thought the message hollow. Perhaps some of those young people thought democracy had already failed them. Why should they bother making "creative effort?"

Dewey's lifelong reflections on democracy and education—reconstructed here—provide the answer. Taking part in the project of pragmatic meliorism within a thriving liberal democratic culture isn't just a chore. It enriches our lives. Our capacities will grow, our experience will be enhanced, as we accept some measure of responsibility for upholding and refining our democratic way of life. The goodness of a flourishing democratic ethos lies in the kinds of characters it forms. In the kinds of lives it makes possible. The grace of ordinary democratic life. The moment when we see one another, as if for the first time. The promise, however tenuous it may seem at times, of pushing back life's boundaries.

There's never been a shortage of naysayers about democratic citizens. We've been told that we will always be blinded by propaganda, stereotype, and prejudice; that we're inherently undisciplined, mediocre, conformist, stupid.[59] Dewey stands out as one of the few serious thinkers who challenged these familiar elitist narratives. This doesn't mean that he ignored our shortcomings. He admitted that mediocrity is real (1922, MW 13:289–94); that prejudice, stereotype, hatred, mistrust are real; that propaganda and other methods of manipulating public opinion are real (1925, LW 2:215). As a pragmatic optimist, he didn't think the problems are insoluble. They aren't our irrevocable fate. A challenge, not a final verdict—that's how we ought to see democracy's current failings. Part of the answer lies in every individual's hands. Another part requires large-scale efforts. Reforming education to strengthen democratic culture is crucial.

Dewey believed in us. Only time will tell if he was right. But to give up is to create a self-fulfilling prophecy. Our efforts "carry the universe forward" (1925, LW 1:214). This is the message of classical American pragmatism, embodied in his writings. Pragmatic optimism isn't blind faith; it is premised on our active involvement in improving life. What Dewey said in 1941 could have been said to us today:

> It is also possible that, after suffering and agony, the change may be for a better society, making possible a freer and more secure life for all. *This better prospect can become an actuality only as our defense takes the form of creative activity to make the democratic way of life a deeper and wider reality than it has been.* . . . We are still a young nation measured in years of existence. We are old in spirit if we cannot once more by the example of our own form of life point out the way in which the nations of the earth can walk in

freedom and cooperative peace. (1941, LW 14:264–65, my emphasis)

As citizens, we need to make our own contributions to the creation of a thriving democratic ethos. As philosophers, we must reflect on the character-forming and culture-shaping influences that can help us do this. This means that education "in its largest sense" (1930, LW 5:289) should, once again, be taken seriously.

3

ART AND EDUCATION

§3.1. THE SUPREME HUMAN INTEREST

Anyone who opens Dewey's *Logic* looking for a treatise on issues that excite contemporary logicians is likely to be disappointed by his apparently bizarre conception of the field. The same is true of his unorthodox aesthetics. *Art as Experience* is a peculiar book. No doubt many modernist art critics, his contemporaries Clive Bell and Roger Fry among them, would have been appalled to see Dewey placing works of fine art on the same continuum with "the tense grace of the ball-player [that] infects the onlooking crowd" and "the delight of the housewife in tending her plants" (1934, LW 10:11). Already in the first few pages of *Art and Experience*, Dewey declares his disagreement with the reigning aestheticians of his day. In their theories,

> Art is remitted to a separate realm, where it is cut off from that association with the materials and aims of every other form of human effort, undergoing, and achievement. A primary task is thus imposed upon one who undertakes to write upon the philosophy of the fine arts. This task is to restore continuity between the refined and intensified forms of experience that are works of

art and the everyday events, doings, and sufferings that are universally recognized to constitute experience. (1934, LW 10:9)

Dewey is probably reacting to *Vision and Design*, Roger Fry's influential manifesto of modernist art criticism, published in 1920. The dialogue is made explicit later in the book: "Mr. Fry is intent upon establishing a radical difference between esthetic values that are intrinsic to things of ordinary experience and the esthetic value with which the artist is concerned" (1934, LW 10:95). It isn't hard to see what worried Dewey. Fry conceived aesthetic experience as demanding "unbiological, disinterested vision" and making "no reference to actual life."[1] In this, Fry was not alone. Roughly at the same time, Clive Bell defended a conception of "pure art with . . . no relation whatever to the significance of life," so essentially and radically divorced from everyday experience that it can never be "a part of daily life."[2] Genuine art must be "remote from the preoccupations and activities of laborious humanity." Only the lucky gifted few can attain "aesthetic exaltation."[3] The rest of us are confined, at best, to second-rate aesthetic pleasures—a dim reflection of the ecstasies of the few. Dewey called such theories of art "esoteric" (1934, LW 10:94). The great American democrat couldn't accept their elitism. They relegated "the mass" of human beings to an impoverished life, devoid of aesthetic pleasures.

Why bother restoring the "lost" continuity? The answer has to do with Dewey's big pragmatic project. Dichotomizing between aesthetic and ordinary experience is an obstacle to human flourishing and development. Overcoming the opposition will enrich our lives.[4] Obviously, this also requires real-world changes: reforming education, enhancing access to the arts for "the mass" of human beings, elevating public life by giving center stage to the arts. *Democracy and Education* envisages increasing scope for creativity and self-expression in educational settings, while a later essay, "Shall We Abolish School Frills? No," takes issue with the idea that "music, drawing, and dramatics" are mere educational "frills" (1933, LW 9:141). *Democracy and Education* also challenges conventional definitions of democratic citizenship and "social efficiency": "*Ability to produce and to enjoy art*, capacity for recreation, the significant utilization of leisure, are more important elements in it [social efficiency] than elements conventionally associated with citizenship" (1916, MW 9:127, my emphasis). And *Art as Experience* advocates placing art at the center of public life—as it was once in ancient Athens.

All this is covered in Dewey's enormous oeuvre. *Art as Experience* lays the theoretical groundwork for the proposals. It advocates a conceptual shift. In place of the "esoteric" (1934, LW 10:94) views put forth by his influential contemporaries, Dewey gives us a new naturalistic aesthetics.

Philosophy, he believed, shouldn't sequester itself from other fields. Theorists of art should draw on insights from psychology, evolutionary biology, anthropology, and socioeconomic analysis.[5] They should investigate art's connection with ordinary human life. They should explore the role that art has played—and may still play—in the development of individuals, communities, and cultures. The book links aesthetic experience to personal growth. And it embeds art in a greater picture of human development, examining "its role in civilization" (1934, LW 10:16).

What is the ultimate goal of the project? Dewey makes it clear:

A conception of fine art that sets out from its connection with discovered qualities of ordinary experience will be able to

indicate the factors and forces that favor the normal development of common human activities into matters of artistic value. It
will also be able to point out those conditions that arrest its normal growth. [. . .] a philosophy of art is sterilized unless it makes
us aware of the function of art in relation to other modes of
experience, and unless it indicates why this function is so inadequately realized, and unless it suggests the conditions under
which the office would be successfully performed (1934, LW
10:17).

Art as Experience follows the procedure laid out in *Experience
and Nature*. Dewey's "empirical method" is twofold. First, it
demands tracing philosophical ideas "back to their origin in primary experience" (1925, LW1:39). *Art as Experience* engages in
this sort of genealogical analysis when it examines (what Dewey
takes to be) the historical and socioeconomic origins of the
dichotomizing between aesthetic experience and everyday life
(e.g., 1934, LW 10:14–15).[6] Second, the method demands testing
philosophies by bringing them "back to the things of ordinary
experience, in all their coarseness and crudity, for verification"
(1925, LW 1:39). *Art as Experience* does this, too. It criticizes the
detrimental real-world effects of "esoteric" theories that isolate
art from the rest of life. Dewey's worry wasn't merely that his
opponents mischaracterized art. Creating a gulf between aesthetic and ordinary experience, he feared, "deeply affects the
practice of living, driving away esthetic perceptions that are necessary ingredients of happiness" (1934, LW 10:16).

Recall the view of the discipline laid out in chapter 1. Philosophy is "a criticism of criticisms" (1925, LW 1:298–99) that
aims to improve special fields, practices, and institutions. It facilitates human development. Art is one of the practices examined
in this vast pragmatic project. *Reconstruction in Philosophy*

explicitly counts the arts among the institutions we should scrutinize based on "their effect in furthering continued education." It tells us that we should examine them afresh with respect to "the contribution they make to the all-round growth of every member of society" (1920, MW 12:186). No reader should be surprised that *Art as Experience* focuses on how the arts enable growth. The book gives us an overarching picture of the relationship between aesthetic experience and human development. It also criticizes defective institutions (e.g., remoteness of museum art, elitist criticism that makes fine art inaccessible to "the mass") that explain why art's growth-enabling potential "is so inadequately realized" (1934, LW 10:17). And it imagines better alternatives (e.g., more creative, active engagement with works of art in museums, 1934, LW 10:17).

In short, *Art as Experience* explores how the arts can "contribute to an expanding and enriched life" (1934, LW 10:34). In this book, too, education broadly conceived as the formation of "fundamental dispositions" serves as a touchstone for philosophical inquiry. By now, the emphasis on growth and human development shouldn't strike the reader as all that strange. It aligns with the idea that philosophy is "the general theory of education" (1916, MW 9:338–39). Dewey's aesthetics is an example of how taking education seriously helps re-orient philosophical inquiry in other fields. In *Art as Experience*, education serves as "the supreme human interest" (1930, LW 5:156) guiding philosophical reflection.

§3.2. DEGRADING ART?

A close reading of the book's opening pages gives us further clues to the uniqueness of the project. Dewey is interested in "being fully alive," being "all there," having "heightened vitality," "complete interpenetration of self and the world of objects and events," "commerce with the world" (1934, LW 10:24–25). The first few chapters set aside "classic" works of art to start afresh. They look at ordinary life to discover how one can be "active through his whole being when he looks and listens" (1934, LW 10:25), to explore "completeness of living in the experience of making and of perceiving," to examine "an experience [of making] in which the whole creature is alive" (1934, LW 10:33). We will give more content to these ideas and supplement them with others as we go along. But it is already clear that Dewey's conception of the aesthetic was nothing like Fry's "unbiological, disinterested vision" that makes "no reference to actual life."[7] Still, Dewey's interpretation of Cézanne and Matisse shows that he thought his theory capable of capturing not only the aesthetic qualities of "the delight of the housewife in tending her plants" (1934, LW 10:11), but also those of modern painting.

"Mountain peaks do not float unsupported; they do not even just rest upon the earth. They are the earth in one of its manifest operations" (1934, LW 10:9). Moments of aesthetic richness—"mountain peaks"—shouldn't be seen as completely disconnected from our career as living beings in this world. They should be seen as particularly vivid manifestations of certain fundamental features of all human experience.

Dewey was well aware that critics might view his approach as "a degrading and Philistinish materialization of works of fine art" (1934, LW 10:17). Connecting art and ordinary experience "may seem to some unworthy" (1934, LW 10:17). Indeed, Dewey's project may raise eyebrows at the very outset. We're told that "in order to understand the meaning of artistic products, we have to forget them for a time, to turn aside from them and have recourse to the ordinary forces and conditions of experience that we do not usually regard as esthetic" (1934, LW 10:10). But why turn to ordinary life? Isn't it often unaesthetic, dull, devoid of the richness we usually associate with fine art? Isn't this why we seek to be in art's presence? Aesthetic experience may help us escape the uninspiring banality of daily life. That is why Fry and Bell held it in such high esteem.

Dewey's project, it might seem, simply misses the mark. As Bell put it, "The value of the greatest art consists not in its power of becoming a part of common existence but in its power of taking us out of it." We needn't agree with Bell's idea that to appreciate art "the most absolute abstraction from the affairs of life is essential," or with his elitist view that aesthetic ecstasy is "incompatible" with the preoccupations of most people. Still, sometimes there is a palpable difference between the richness of experience given to us by works of art and the dullness of what we usually call ordinary life. Perhaps Bell's esoteric rhetoric was a legitimate expression of contempt for "the smug materialism" and conventionality of modern industrial societies.[8] Everyday life under the current socioeconomic conditions can be routine, confining, unaesthetic. Why not see fine art as "alien" to this sort of life? Is Dewey oblivious to the problem when he turns to "ordinary experience" in search of the aesthetic? Is he unaware of the potential tensions?

I think not. *Experience and Nature* acknowledges the issue: "The existence of activities that have no immediate enjoyed intrinsic meaning is undeniable. They include much of our labors in home, factory, laboratory and study. By no stretch of language can they be termed either artistic or esthetic" (1925, LW 1:271–72). This is echoed in *Art as Experience*: "If artistic and esthetic quality is implicit in every normal experience, how shall we explain how and why it so generally fails to become explicit?" (1934, LW 10:18) Dewey was a perceptive critic of the shape that human experience takes in modern capitalist societies. To criticize and reimagine the existing institutions—precisely because daily life is often so stunted, meaningless, mechanical—was his task. His unorthodox aesthetics was part of that project.

A distinction between different senses of "ordinary experience" can help us here. (Dewey never made it explicitly. But it allows us to make sense of his position.) The phrase might refer to the sort of experience most people ordinarily have under the current socioeconomic conditions. Alternatively, it might refer to the sort of experience that "ordinary" human beings—as opposed to artists—are capable of having; the sort of experience that we can have in "ordinary" circumstances (for instance, in a conversation with a friend—and not just at an art gallery); the sort of experience that isn't "super-human," supernatural, esoteric.

Now the pragmatist's approach appears more palatable. Dewey didn't argue that all experience under the current socioeconomic conditions should be placed on the same level as that offered to us by fine art.[9] Quite the contrary. He was a vehement critic of the confinement and dullness of industrial capitalism. And yet he didn't share the elitism of those who thought that ordinary people are incapable of enjoying the aesthetic. Nor did he think that the aesthetic must necessarily exclude all other human concerns (our passions, desires, life histories).[10]

Much of our experience may be routine and dull (1934, LW 10:110). But ordinary life also contains some moments of richness when we feel "fully alive." Rare and transient as they may be, these moments may illuminate directions for improvement. They aren't signs of a "super-human" ecstasy that descends on us from on high. They are natural outcomes of our interactions with our physical and social environments. If we examine the conditions and consequences of these rich experiences, we can improve our life on the individual and social levels. We can make such rich experiences more prevalent. Eventually, they may even come to define our daily lives.

So perhaps Dewey's project wasn't completely misguided. Still, I have not yet provided a full answer to the worry that it "degrades" art. Even granting that Dewey didn't attempt to defend the daily life of most human beings under the prevailing socioeconomic conditions as wholly aesthetic, we still need a further story about his notion of "ordinary experience." We need to find out what, on his view, accounts for the alleged continuity. The debate with Fry will serve as a helpful entry point into Dewey's complex position. As we shall see, growth—education "in its largest sense"—is central to the picture.

§3.3. TO BUILD A RICHER PERSONALITY

Dewey's attitude toward Fry's work was complex. Like Fry, he appreciated modern nonrepresentational painting. The pragmatist even praised Fry for his sophisticated analysis of how an artist fascinated by the beauty of lines and colors transforms her vision into abstract art. It is, Dewey said, "an excellent account of the sort of thing that takes place in artistic perception and creation" (1934, LW 10:93). What he took issue with was the critic's tendency to divorce aesthetic from ordinary experience (1934, LW 10:95).

How did he respond to Fry? By interrogating the specific terms in which the modernist critic tried to capture aesthetic experience. Dewey wanted to show that it isn't radically disconnected from the aesthetic features present (in however incipient a form) in ordinary life. To do this, he tried to re-describe the process. *Art as Experience* does this in Dewey's favorite terms, inspired by evolutionary biology and psychology. It tells us that the artist's vision is an interaction of an organism with its environment. In the process, the organism draws on adaptations from previous experiences. And it develops itself further. Dewey resisted the idea that the artist's vision can ever be wholly "pure." It cannot be completely disconnected from her life history, habits, and predispositions. It cannot be totally divorced from the "background of experiences" that have shaped her:

> The painter did not approach the scene with an empty mind, but with a background of experiences long ago funded into capacities and likes, or with a commotion due to more recent experiences. He comes with a mind waiting, patient, willing to be impressed and yet not without bias and tendency in vision. Hence lines and color crystallize in this harmony rather than in that. This especial mode of harmonization is *not the exclusive result of the lines and colors. It is a function of what is in the actual scene in its interaction with what the beholder brings with him. Some subtle affinity with the current of his own experience as a live creature* causes lines and colors to arrange themselves in one pattern and rhythm rather than in another. (1934, LW 10:93, my emphasis)

Two features of artistic vision (as Dewey conceived it) stand out here. First, as mentioned earlier, it is an interaction of the live creature with its environment. Second, the artist approaches the world with organs of vision shaped by past experience. This happens at a specific point in her life history. At that instant, certain features of reality—for example, specific relationships of line and color that have "affinities" with the current of her experience—speak vividly to her. The notion of "timeless," "pure" aesthetic vision is a myth.[11]

Genuine aesthetic vision, on Fry's view, is "unbiological," "disinterested."[12] In this process, "inner material" (1934, LW 10:81)—including that developed in prior experiences—seems to have no place. The view was amplified by other influential critics of Dewey's day. Bell wrote that "to appreciate a work of art we need bring with us nothing from life, no knowledge of its ideas and affairs, no familiarity with its emotions."[13] As Dewey saw it, the view was too restrictive. It mischaracterized aesthetic experience. There is no "empty," "pure" vision. The perceiver interacts with what she sees. In this process, she might move beyond her former ways of seeing. She might succeed in appreciating something new. But this vision isn't utterly disengaged from all her habits and impulses. It isn't completely unrelated to her past and future. In fact, it can have a profound influence on the rest of her life. Dewey believed that art and aesthetic experience may help each of us "build a richer personality" (1934, LW 10:252–53). This is true for both artist and audience.[14]

Artistic activity isn't about expressing a self that has already been completely formed. The self cannot be "regarded as something complete and self-contained in isolation" (1934, LW 10:112). Creative activity helps fashion it: "the self is created in the creation of objects" (1934, LW 10:287). As the artist shapes her material in some definite medium, the self also develops: "the expression of the self in and through a medium, constituting the work of art, is *itself* a prolonged interaction of something issuing from the self with objective conditions, a process in which *both* of them acquire a form and order *they did not at first possess*" (1934, LW 10:71, my emphases). This crucial point connects Dewey's aesthetics to the account of cultivating individuality in *Experience and Nature*. We are starting to get a glimpse of the connection between creativity and personal growth.

That the artist shapes her material—marble, paint, words—is obvious. What is less often recognized is that this process simultaneously transforms the creator (1934, LW 10:81–82). *"The work is artistic in the degree in which the two functions of transformation are effected by a single operation.* As the painter places pigment upon the canvas, or imagines it placed there, *his ideas and feeling are also ordered.* As the writer composes in his medium of words what he wants to say, his idea takes on for himself perceptible form" (1934, LW 10:81–82, my emphases).

This has to be explained in more depth. What exactly is it in the "self" that is being transformed? Dewey isn't particularly clear on this point. Some passages suggest that the "meanings and values" developed in prior experiences are reshaped in artistic endeavor (1934, LW 10:95). Other passages focus on "inner materials" consisting of "images, observations, memories and emotions," "ideas and feelings" (1934, LW 10:81–82). We are also told that "the impulsion," "the inner commotion" that motivates the expressive act is managed in some way. It gains some shape as we express it. This, too, is part of the "inner material" that is being transfigured in the creative act. Still other passages suggest that aesthetic experience alters the "schemes" through which we see the world (1934, LW 10:110).

When they are expressed in "outward" material, inchoate needs and impulses are clarified and defined. The stock of "inner material" developed in the past is also altered. *Art as Experience* defines "aesthetic emotion" in terms of the artist's refashioning of self and world: "It is precisely this transformation that changes the character of the original emotion, altering its quality so that it becomes *distinctively esthetic in nature*" (1934, LW 10:82, my emphasis).

Unsurprisingly, the book explicitly connects this sort of reshaping with Dewey's favorite concept—growth (1934, LW

10:65). Here, too, the notion remains central to the pragmatist's project. *Art as Experience* begins with the suggestion that the "biological commonplaces" of growth "reach to the roots of the esthetic in experience" (1934, LW 10:19). In response to one of his critics, Dewey indicated that what links *Art as Experience* to the rest of his oeuvre is "the principle of development that holds so universally in my theory of a variety of phases of experience such as morals, politics, religion, science, philosophy itself, as well as the fine arts" (1949, LW 16:397). This principle is growth. Unfortunately, Dewey wasn't especially clear about how growth connects to aesthetic experience. We need to reconstruct the picture from a number of hints scattered throughout his works. To makes sense of the view, *Art as Experience* needs to be read alongside other works—*Human Nature and Conduct*, *Democracy and Education*, "Creative Democracy." This will allow us to grasp Dewey's position on how the arts enhance the self. As we shall see, they help remake our habits, developing our ability to engage with and appreciate the world around us. This doesn't just affect our perception of the physical environment. Among other things, we can also grow in how we relate to others.

Dewey's psychology was inspired by William James, who recognized the role that habit and selective attention pay in shaping our perception: "*the only things which we commonly see are those which we preperceive*, and the only things which we preperceive are those which have been labelled for us, and the labels stamped into our mind."[15] However, human beings are not forever doomed to being stuck within their current field of vision. We are capable of revising our habits and of developing our characters. James's tone is therefore not one of fatalism but of exhilaration at the richness of possibilities opened up by his suggestion that we may "carve" reality in different ways. Like James, Dewey believed that habits affect our sensations, ideas, and thoughts. They constitute our virtues, vices, and characters (1922, MW 14:25). Habits may be useful, but they may also become "routine" (1916, MW 9:53). Rigid and inflexible habits can get us stuck in ruts, foreclosing possibilities. They may prevent us from experiencing the richness of the world around us. Sometimes, they even limit our ability to engage with and communicate with others (1934, LW 10:110). The limitations of relying on routine habits are already prefigured in James's *Principles*: "men have no eyes but for those aspects of things which they have already been taught to discern."[16] Dewey adds to the account: rigid, unexamined, routine habits may stifle human development and flourishing. At their worst, they turn into prejudices, such as racial and gender stereotypes (1922, MW 13:248). The worry about routine habits, already articulated in *Democracy and Education*, is echoed in *Art as Experience*. Art helps us break through such obstacles: "art quickens us from the slackness of routine" (1934, LW 10:110).

Recall the explanation of Deweyan growth offered in chapter 2. Growth is a fundamental feature of life. Understood at the most general level (in a way that applies to all living things), growth occurs when an organism adjusts to a novel or disruptive stimulus in such a way as to increase the organism's overall capacity to solve problems likely to arise for it (although there may be some losses) (1916, MW 9:4). This process may involve changing the environment and (for higher-level organisms) may issue in new habits that direct future activity. Since habits help define our characters, personal growth can be understood as a process of character formation whereby we acquire a greater ability to appreciate and interact with the physical and social world.

We can now refine the distinction offered earlier. The phrase "ordinary experience" could be taken to refer to the daily life of most human beings under the current socioeconomic conditions (which may in fact provide few opportunities for growth). Alternatively, it could be taken to refer to life that exhibits growth. When Dewey defends the aesthetic richness of ordinary life, it's the second sense he has in mind. Deweyan growth isn't open only to the few intellectuals or artists. It isn't something "esoteric" or "supra-human." Growth is part of "ordinary life" as Dewey understood it.

And it is central to human flourishing.

§3.4. RAIN CLOUDS AND CATHEDRALS

Now we're starting to get a more elaborate picture of how Dewey connected education and aesthetic experience. As he saw it, art may help us grow by pushing us beyond the limits of our current habits of perception and action. As a result, we may develop habits that allow richer and fuller engagement with the physical and social environment.[17] The distinction between genuine aesthetic perception and mere recognition sheds further light on Dewey's position:

> In recognition we fall back, as upon a stereotype, upon some previously formed scheme. Some detail or arrangement of details serves as cue for bare identification. It suffices in recognition to apply this bare outline as a stencil to the present object. Sometimes in contact with a human being we are struck with traits, perhaps of only physical characteristics, of which we were not previously aware. We realize that we never knew the person before; we had not seen him in any pregnant sense. We now begin to study and to "take in." Perception replaces bare recognition. There is an act of reconstructive doing, and consciousness becomes fresh and alive. (1934, LW 10:59)

Recognition relies exclusively on already formed habits. When an existing pattern is applied to the thing identified, the process ends. No further work takes place. By contrast, perception is creative. When we make an effort to look more carefully, our existing schemes may be transformed and our experience enriched. Art may enhance our capacity to perceive and interact with "the world of things and persons" (1925, LW 1:188): "Familiarity induces indifference, prejudice blinds us; conceit looks through the wrong end of a telescope. . . . Art throws off the covers that hide the expressiveness of experienced things; it quickens us from the slackness of routine and enables us to forget ourselves by finding ourselves in the delight of experiencing the world about us in varied qualities and forms (1934, LW 10:110)."

The distinction between recognition and perception is developed in two other sets of passages (1934, LW 10:181–82 and 223–24). In "Art as Experience," we're told that the aesthetic object is "built up" in perception. In Dewey's process-oriented theory, aesthetic objects aren't static entities independent of the observer. They develop in the interaction of the perceiver with the environment: "perception and its object are built up and completed in one and the same continuing operation" (1934, LW 10:181–82). How does this relate to what was said earlier? Here, too, Dewey is concerned that automatically applying preconceived schemes in acts of mere recognition "cuts short" aesthetic objects:

> Now under the pressure of external circumstances or because of internal laxity, objects of most of our ordinary perception lack completeness. They are cut short when there is recognition; that is to say when the object is identified as one of a kind, or of a species within the kind. For such recognition suffices to enable us to employ the object for customary purposes. It is enough to know that those objects are rain-clouds to induce us to carry an umbrella.

The full perceptual realization of just the individual clouds they are might even get in the way of utilizing them as an index of a specific, a limited, kind of conduct. Esthetic perception, on the other hand, is a name for a full perception and its correlative, an object or event. Such a perception is accompanied by, or rather consists in, a release of energy in its purest form. (1934, LW 10:181–82)

In instances of recognition, we classify objects as belonging to a certain kind or species. (Presumably, this happens when we apply some preconceived scheme.) We need to move beyond this sort of rigid classification in an effort to see unique features of the object. A hasty observer interested only in whether she needs an umbrella is satisfied when she classifies the clouds in the sky as rain clouds. Genuine aesthetic perception must go further.

There's something troubling about this passage. How do we know that our perception is "full?" Isn't there a sense in which it's never complete? Indeed, numerous passages in *Art as Experience* acknowledge the "inexhaustibility" of works of art (e.g., 1934, LW 10:223). We are told that works of art "continuously inspire new personal realizations in experience" (1934, LW 10:113–14), that "there is no final term in appreciation of a work of art" (1934, LW 10:144). This seems to be in tension with the idea that perception—and aesthetic objects—can ever be "complete." I will discuss this worry in more depth in my concluding remarks. For now, I suggest a meliorist revision of Dewey's understanding of aesthetic perception. Even if it can never be truly complete, it can be fuller, richer. We can develop aesthetic objects *further* than we usually do. Hastily glancing at the clouds with an umbrella in hand isn't enough. We need to explore their unique shapes and colors in an effort to see things we had never noticed before.

Dewey invokes an experience we're all familiar with—rushing by a beautiful architectural landmark or landscape:

> A cathedral, no matter how large, makes an instantaneous impression. . . . But this is only the substratum and framework within which a continuous process of interactions introduces enriching and defining elements. The hasty sightseer no more has an esthetic vision of Saint Sophia or the Cathedral of Rouen than the motorist traveling at sixty miles an hour sees the flitting landscape. One must move about, within and without, and through repeated visits let the structure gradually yield itself to him in various lights and in connection with changing moods. (1934, LW 10:223–24)

The example is aptly chosen. Though the passage makes no mention of Monet, the carelessness of Dewey's "hasty sightseer" can be easily contrasted with the great impressionist's extraordinary "research" in painting his famous *Cathedral of Rouen* series. To capture it, Monet believed, he had to look at the cathedral under all possible lighting conditions: the pinks of early dawn, the glaring light of noon, the flaming yellows of the sunset, the blues of gathering dusk. One painting simply couldn't do it justice. He painted twenty. Working simultaneously on multiple canvases, Monet kept chasing the ephemeral effects of light and color that played across the cathedral's facade.[18]

The artist's letters testify to the astonishing seriousness with which he approached his task. They echo Dewey's idea that aesthetic perception opens up unappreciated aspects of the world: "each day I discover things which I did not see the day before."[19] Always his own harshest reviewer, Monet felt humbled by the richness of his subject: "What is it that's taken hold of me, for me to carry on like this in relentless pursuit of something beyond my powers?"[20] The critic Virginia Spate suggests he saw painting "as an investigative process."[21] To the self-doubting Monet, it seemed never-ending: "I have now taken up so singular a way of working that I work vainly, it doesn't seem to advance at all."[22] But the effort was worth it. Seeking to do justice to his subject, Monet abandoned many painterly conventions of his time.[23] The result was a stunning series that offered a new mode of vision. His Rouen Cathedral was no longer just another specimen of Gothic architecture.[24] It was the outcome of what Dewey called genuine aesthetic perception.[25] Pissarro admired the "research" behind the twenty canvases: "it's above all as an ensemble that it should be seen. It's much opposed by the young and even by admirers of Monet. I'm very excited by this extraordinary mastery. Cézanne . . . fully agrees with me that it's the work of a strong-willed, level-headed man, pursuing the ungraspable nuances of effects which I don't see realized by any other artist. . . . Personally, I find any research legitimate if it's felt to this degree."[26]

From a Deweyan perspective, what happened when Monet engaged in genuine perception was twofold. On the one hand, the object (in this instance, the cathedral) was "developed," "built up" further than it would have been in acts of mere recognition. The painter's habits were also reconstructed as he learned to appreciate new aspects of reality. Dewey believed this isn't just true for artists. It is also true for creative, properly engaged consumers of art (more on this below). Among other things, engaging with the *Cathedral of Rouen* painting series expands our capacity to appreciate subtle effects of light and color in settings far beyond the art gallery.

Though Dewey doesn't explicitly say so in the passages we have considered so far, he would surely have agreed that there is a third aspect to the growth accompanying this sort of work.

Experience and Nature already hints at it. Artistic "innovations and deviations . . . reshape the world of objects and institutions" (1925, LW 1:188). Monet's work doesn't just help individuals learn to see new aspects of reality. It also adds to the repertoire of subjects, techniques, and perspectives on which future artists may draw. As an institution, art is reshaped.

This last point aligns with Dewey's celebration of modern painting toward the end of *Art as Experience*: "The bathing beaches, street corners, flowers and fruits, babies and bankers of contemporary painting are . . . the fruits of a new vision" (1934, LW 10:342–43). What modern painters achieved is of enduring value: "the extension of painting and the other arts to include matter that was once regarded as either too common or too out of the way to deserve artistic recognition is a permanent gain" (1934, LW 10:343). Monet's painstaking rendition of the most ephemeral, "ungraspable nuances" of light and color is a "permanent gain," too.[27]

§3.5. ARTIST AND AUDIENCE

All this illuminates the first of the two conceptual revisions I want to highlight. The artist's activity doesn't involve "pure," "disinterested," "timeless" vision. It engages and enriches her self, the "inner material" formed in the past. The second conceptual revision I want to emphasize supplements the first. "What is true of the producer is true of the perceiver" (1934, LW 10:113). The perceiver must create her own experience (1934, LW 10:61). This, too, develops the self. *Art as Experience* seeks to break down the rigid distinction between producers and consumers of art. It suggests that properly engaging with art (and, more generally, engaging with things and persons in a creative way) educates us. It helps us grow.

But is the work done by the audience identical to the artist's efforts? This doesn't seem right. Dewey isn't particularly careful on this point. We might object that the consumer engages with something that is quite different from the scene in front of the artist. Delightful as it is, looking at Monet's *Cathedral of Rouen* paintings isn't the same as exploring the actual Cathedral of Rouen.[28] A charitable reading suggests a weaker claim. Both producers and (properly engaged) consumers of art are creative. Both assimilate something new to past experience. Both reconstruct existing habits. Both learn to appreciate additional aspects of life. Monet may have done all this while conducting the meticulous "research" that revealed the most subtle effects of light playing across the cathedral's facade. I might do this by looking at his paintings. But our activities are not identical.

The weaker reading aligns nicely with another important point. A strict identity of response between producer and consumer doesn't leave enough room for the audience's creativity. *Art as Experience* tells us that "works of art" are incitements to further creative activity on the part of perceivers, in which the actual "work" of art is done (1934, LW 10:9). Far from being "monotonously" identical "throughout the ages" (1934, LW 10:113–14), a work of art is great to the extent that it inspires us to perform further creative acts.

Rilke's reworking of the imagery from Picasso's *La famille des saltimbanques* is a good example. The poet "spent the summer and early fall of 1915 living beside 'the great Picasso'" at a friend's apartment. The acrobats in the painting inspired the imagery in his *Fifth Duino Elegy*. "The great Picasso" resonated with Rilke's own life: his persistent sense of homelessness and alienation, his anxiety about his calling, his feeling of being overpowered by psychic forces not under his control.[29] Of course, not all consumption of art must result in literally new artworks. Perhaps Rilke's engagement with *La famille des saltimbanques* lies at one extreme of a continuum in which we can locate other (more modest yet still enriching) instances of audience creativity.

The line between consuming and creating art isn't as clearcut as we usually assume. Properly engaging with art isn't just about assimilating it to some preconceived interpretive scheme (e.g., classifying *La famille des saltimbanques* as an early Picasso). It requires connecting art to our own lived experience. In the poet's eyes, Picasso's painting was "remade afresh"—just as Dewey envisaged.

As the pragmatist saw it, the actual work of art isn't an object isolated from us (1934, LW 10:113–14). It's a process that engages the self. One that continues, ever afresh, in each person's encounter with the object. Some artworks, like Picasso's *La famille des saltimbanques*, are particularly suggestive (at least to some people).[30] They "continuously inspire new personal realizations in experience" (1934, LW 10:113–14).[31] Ever new experiences of such works transform us as we develop them. Their value doesn't lie in some detached, complete significance. Nor does it lie in their "aloofness" from our characters and lives. It lies in art's educative potential, in its ability to speak to us, provoking the desire to do the real work of art for ourselves. As Marcel Proust once eloquently put it, "The supreme effort of the writer as of the artist only succeeds in raising partially for us the veil of ugliness and insignificance that leaves us incurious before the universe. Then does he say: 'Look, look . . . at the house in Zeeland pink and shiny as a seashell. *Look! Learn to see!*' *At which moment he disappears.*"[32] Dewey's view was similar. Encounters with works of art are incitements to keep growing. This couldn't be further from Bell's idea that the "universality" of great works of art resides in some "stable" significance completely "independent of time and place" and "as independent as mathematical truth of human vicissitudes."[33]

§3.6. USEFUL IN THE ULTIMATE DEGREE

How does this illuminate Dewey's response to Fry? The modernist critic was worried that the field of human vision is narrowed down by "ordinary life" and by "utility:"

> Biologically speaking, art is a blasphemy. . . . We have learned the meaning for life of appearances so well that we understand them, as it were, in shorthand. The subtlest differences of appearance that have a utility value still continue to be appreciated, while large and important visual characters, provided they are useless for life, will pass unnoticed. . . . Some of us can tell Canadian Cheddar at a glance, and no one was ever taken in by sham suede gloves. . . . So we learn to read the prophetic message, and, for the sake of economy, to neglect all else. Children have not learned it fully, and so they look at things with some passion. Even the grown man keeps something of his unbiological, disinterested vision with regard to a few things. He still looks at flowers, and does not merely see them.[34]

In many ways Fry's approach was deeply at odds with Dewey's. Claiming that "biologically speaking, art is a blasphemy" immediately sets aesthetic experience apart from our activities as biological organisms. Dewey sought to connect the two. As Fry saw it, true art is inimical to "utility." The pragmatist wanted to establish the opposite.

But a careful reading suggests the two may have shared some underlying concerns. Closely examining the reasons why Fry opposed connecting art to "biological vision" and to "utility" reveals a more nuanced picture. Fry wanted to defend a radically new mode of artistic vision, exemplified in modernist nonrepresentational painting. He worried that "life" and "the useful" (e.g., distinguishing sham suede gloves from real ones) narrow down the field of our vision, preventing us from appreciating aesthetic features captured in modern painting. A telling detail is Fry's distinction between "seeing" and "looking." "Mere seeing" ("biological" and "interested") is seeing things "in shorthand." In other words, it is seeing only those aspects of reality that are immediately useful to us and ignoring all else. "Looking" is a richer activity that seeks to push beyond the limits of such impoverished "seeing." "Looking" discloses features of reality that may have been obscured by automatic, habitual identification of lines and colors with specific objects. Nonrepresentational art teaches us to "look" at things afresh.

Perhaps Fry and Dewey weren't utterly at odds, after all. In fact, Dewey's understanding of genuinely aesthetic experience (as opposed to mere recognition) seems to have some unexpected affinities with Fry's view. But Dewey offers us a very different way of describing the process. He interprets genuine aesthetic perception—including the sort celebrated by Fry—in terms of a modification of habits. This refashioning is embedded in the processes central to (what Dewey thinks of as) "ordinary" life. And it is educative "in the largest sense."

From a Deweyan perspective, Fry's mistake is to assume that pushing beyond the boundaries of our habitual ways of seeing is "unbiological," radically disconnected from (and necessarily useless with respect to) our other activities. Dewey talks about "utilizing" aesthetic objects for "customary purposes," in a "limited" way (1934, LW 10:181–82). He recognizes that glancing at rain clouds with the sole purpose of telling the weather isn't going to generate an enriching aesthetic experience. This doesn't mean, however, that all artistic vision must necessarily be completely useless. Dewey offers us a broader conception of usefulness. On this conception, the enrichment of experience that occurs in aesthetic perception is supremely useful. Aesthetic perception is at once "consummatory" and "instrumental" (1925, LW 1:274). In disclosing new aspects of the world to us, it makes our experience immediately richer. And it enhances future experience by remaking our ways of interacting with the world. For instance, engaging with Monet's *Cathedral of Rouen* series can resonate throughout one's life as one gains a greater capacity to appreciate evanescent effects of light.

Dewey's expansive conception of usefulness goes far beyond narrowly "utilitarian" ends. To be sure, the usefulness of art doesn't lie in helping us tell sham suede gloves from real ones. But art enriches our present and future experience. It develops our characters. It enhances our community life as we become more sympathetic toward others. All this makes art "useful in the ultimate degree—that of contributing directly and liberally to an expanding and enriched life" (1934, LW 10:33–34). The usefulness of art lies in its educative and enriching quality.

Dewey shared Fry's concern that certain kinds of interestedness (e.g., wondering whether one needs an umbrella, 1934, LW 10:181–82) cut short aesthetic perception. Yet he didn't conclude that artistic vision should be entirely "disinterested."[35] Certainly, when an abstract painter creates a work of art, her interests aren't narrowly "utilitarian." She might be satisfying "the hunger of the eyes for light and color" (1934, LW 10:130). On the other end, the perceiver might be interested in pushing beyond the boundaries of her habitual vision when she explores shapes and colors in a nonrepresentational painting. But none of this activity is "pure" in Fry's or Bell's sense. It's not completely detached from life. The educative processes of growth are central to Dewey's conception of "ordinary" life. Grasping this takes us beyond narrow conceptions of utility.

Now we can respond to the worry raised earlier. We needn't fear that Dewey's effort to restore the "lost" continuity between art and ordinary life degrades the latter. His conception of life gives central place to the growth occurring we go beyond our day-to-day preoccupations to appreciate some hitherto neglected aspects of reality. Sometimes this involves learning to see the beauty of lines and colors captured in modern painting.

Bell was intent on setting "aesthetic exaltation" apart from life.[36] From a Deweyan naturalistic perspective, this approach appears misguided. Dewey would have said that it's the enrichment that accompanies growth that accounts (at least partially) for the "exaltation." Recall the passages where he talks about "being fully alive" (1934, LW 10:24), having "heightened vitality" (1934, LW 10:25), about consciousness becoming fresh and alive (1934, LW 10:59). Moreover, Dewey's perspective suggests a greater continuity between the enrichment that occurs when we engage with fine art and the enrichment involved in other creative activities—creative friendship, creative citizenship, even creative gardening.[37] The attempt to break down the rigid barrier between fine arts and the creative, enriching activities of "ordinary" life is already prefigured in *Experience and Nature*: "Any activity that is productive of objects whose perception is an immediate good, and whose operation is a continual source of enjoyable perception of other events *exhibits the fineness of art*" (1925, LW 1:274, my emphasis).[38]

For Dewey, the crucial distinction wasn't between the arts of living and the fine arts. What he really cared about was drawing a line between activities pursued in a mechanical, routine, uncreative manner that limits our development—and growth-enabling ones. The idea that growth is a fundamental feature of life (not something "super-human") helps Dewey make his favorite move. It helps him break down rigid dichotomizing between the fine arts and the arts of life (friendship, citizenship, work). Of course, he recognized that the daily life of many human beings isn't growth-enabling. The plight of the factory worker forced mechanically to produce objects according to a preset scheme resonated deeply with Dewey's concerns. As did the existence of prejudices that confine us (1922, MW 13:244; 1934, LW 10:110).

That is why many of his works call for reforms to enrich human lives. This is especially true of his reflections on schooling. Once we appreciate their growth-enabling potential, we see clearly why adding the arts (and other creative activities) to school curricula isn't just a useless extravagance.

"Shall we abolish school 'frills?'" (1933, LW 9:141). The question is as urgent today as it was in Dewey's time. Critics of educational "frills" see them as luxuries, dispensable in times of economic crisis. Defenders view them as central to human flourishing.[39] The debate isn't new. In depression-era America, skeptics already argued against spending taxpayer money on enhancing public education with "music, drawing, and dramatics" (1933, LW 9:141).[40] Dewey disagreed. The arts (and other subjects offering creative opportunities) shouldn't be a luxury for the few (1933, LW 9:141–46).[41] They are integral to "a life worth living" (1920, MW 12:200–201).

He even went so far as to say that a critic "who is active in attacking our schools because of their 'frills' . . . disbelieves in the whole democratic endeavor" (1933, LW 9:142). This striking indictment reveals the vastness of the "democratic social experiment" (1933, LW 9:141) as Dewey conceived it. The Deweyan democratic project involves giving all human beings access to creative, growth-enabling pursuits.[42] That is why his 1933 essay rejects "schools for the masses that confine education to a few simple and mechanical skills" (1933, LW 9:145). That is why *Democracy and Education* argues against limiting public education to "the three R's" (1916, MW 9:200)

The theme runs as a central thread through his extensive oeuvre: already in 1897, the young Dewey mused on the importance of aesthetic education (1897, EW 5:202–3). But it wasn't until 1934 that Dewey formulated his aesthetic theory in full (1934, LW 10). Even Dewey's pragmatic manifesto, *Reconstruction in Philosophy*, ends with a plea for enhancing the aesthetic richness of ordinary life:

> When the liberation of capacity no longer seems a menace to organization and established institutions . . . when the liberating of human capacity operates as a socially creative force, *art will not be a luxury*, a stranger to the daily occupations of making a living. Making a living economically speaking, will be at one with making a life that is worth living. And when the emotional force, the mystic force one might say, of communication, of the miracle of shared life and shared experience is spontaneously felt, the hardness and crudeness of contemporary life will be bathed in the light that never was on land or sea. (1920, MW 12:200–201, my emphasis)

Still, skeptics might object that those who defend school "frills" need a more detailed account of their educative value. Dewey's 1933 essay, "Shall We Abolish School 'Frills?' No," doesn't tell us enough. He claims that "music, drawing, and dramatics" (1933, LW 9:141) aren't useless indulgences. But he doesn't say anything specific about their effect on human development and flourishing. My reconstruction of his aesthetics in *Art as Experience* provides the rest of the answer on Dewey's behalf. The arts (and other subjects that foster creativity) enable personal growth, developing our characters, transforming the way we see the world and one another. And they can do more still. The creativity and sympathy developed in such activities prepare us for citizenship in its broadest sense. They prepare us to improve and enrich our democratic life as we engage in a sympathetic and open-minded dialogue.

§3.7. THE SUFFERING AND JOY OF OTHERS

The example I have been focusing on up to now, Monet's *Cathedral of Rouen* series, isn't fully representative, for it doesn't shed much light on another crucial aspect of Dewey's view.[43] The growth accompanying aesthetic experience isn't limited to expanding our appreciation of hidden visual characteristics. The process may change how we engage with others, widening the scope of our sympathy and human understanding. A passage quoted earlier hints at this side of the story. It suggests that genuine perception might involve reconstructing the image of another human being: "We realize that we never knew the person before; we had not seen him in any pregnant sense. We now begin to study and to 'take in.' Perception replaces bare recognition. There is an act of reconstructive doing" (1934, LW 10:59). Such acts of creative, transformative perception are central to life in a thriving Deweyan democracy. They allow us to go beyond the prejudices that confine us. We grow as we learn to see each other anew.[44]

Dewey saw art as the purest form of communication: "The expressions that constitute art are communication in its pure and undefiled form" (1934, LW 10:248–49). And it's particularly effective: "works of art are *the only media of complete and unhindered communication* between man and man that can occur in a world full of gulfs and walls that limit community of experience" (1934, LW 10:110, my emphasis). Elsewhere, we're told that all genuine communication requires that we find points of contact with the lives of others:

> To formulate [experience] requires getting outside of it, seeing it as another would see it, considering what points of contact it has with the life of another so that it may be got into such form that he can appreciate its meaning. Except in dealing with commonplaces and catch phrases one has to assimilate, imaginatively, something of another's experience in order to tell him intelligently of one's own experience. (1916, MW 9:8–9)

An especially rich and effective form of communication, art "enables us to share vividly and deeply in meanings to which we had been dumb" (1934, LW 10:248–49). It helps us become more sensitive to the suffering and joy of others, which is why Dewey admired Tolstoy's novels (ca. 1910–11, LW 17:381). The psychologist Ellen Winner has disputed the claim that engaging with art enhances general sympathy.[45] But this sort of skepticism doesn't undermine the claim that art enhances our sympathy for specific human predicaments (or for specific features of human experience present in otherwise different lives). Even if it doesn't develop some "generalized" skill of sympathy, engaging with other lives in works of art expands our repertoire of human understanding.

One might think here of Rilke's poems. They often inhabit overlooked perspectives—the homeless, the poor, the blind, children—seeking to give voice to the suffering of those who would otherwise remain voiceless, shunned by modern societies: "And, since otherwise people will pass them by *the way they pass things*, they have to sing."[46] The poems don't just disclose suffering. They celebrate the beauty, dignity, and strength of these neglected lives. *The Book of Poverty and Death* envisages a world in which "the poor are no longer / despised and thrown away. / Look at them standing about—/ like wildflowers, which have nowhere else to grow." In his incandescent poems, their predicaments are reimagined in ways that challenge prejudice and indifference: "Evicted from wherever they lived, / they wander the night like ghosts, / . . . If there exists a mouth for their protection, may it open now and speak." Rilke's sensitivity to the suffering and richness of other lives, his ability to look at the world from underestimated vantage points, was extraordinary. And it wasn't limited to human beings. His poetry explores "the suffering of birds on freezing nights, / of dogs who go hungry for days. / . . . the long sad waiting of animals / who are locked up and forgotten."[47]

Reading Rilke extends our sympathy for specific human predicaments—those of the homeless, the poor, the blind, children.[48] And it does still more. It helps create a new vocabulary and a new narrative for those whom our society treats as outcasts. For, in Rilke's poetry, "each being is cleaner than washed stones."[49] There is, as Dewey envisaged, "an act of reconstructive doing," "we realize that we never knew the person before; we had not seen him in any pregnant sense" (1934, LW 10:59). Inhabiting overlooked perspectives, Rilke holds up a mirror to modern life.[50] Engaging with his work doesn't just extend our sympathy. The voices of outcasts in Rilke's poetry challenge us to reconsider how we should live: "We are shunned as if contaminated, / thrown away like broken pots, like bones, / like last year's calendar. / And yet if our Earth needed to / she could weave us together like roses / and make of us a garland."[51]

Dewey wasn't alone in recognizing art's ability to help us overcome prejudices, extending our appreciation and sympathy to overlooked human predicaments. W. E. B. Du Bois's *The Souls of Black Folk* is at once a powerful example of art that enables this kind of growth—and a philosophical reflection on its importance in the context of racial oppression: "Herein the longing of black men must have respect: the rich and bitter depth of their experience, the unknown treasures of their inner life, the strange rendings of nature they have seen, may give the world new points of view and make their loving, living, and doing precious to all human hearts." The phrase "the rich and bitter depth of their experience" beautifully captures the book's tone. Du Bois doesn't limit himself to illuminating the suffering and injustice of racial oppression. He also shows us the richness and beauty of African American lives, their "unknown treasures," opening up "new points of view."[52] This is echoed in other works. "Of Beauty and Death," a chapter in Du Bois's autobiographical *Darkwater*, explores both the ugliness of racism and the magnificence of Du Bois's aesthetic encounters with the Grand Canyon and Montego Bay.[53] "Between the sterner flights of logic," Du Bois tells us, "I have sought to set some little alightings of what may be poetry. They are tributes to Beauty."[54] Extending our sympathy and appreciation provokes us to think about how we should live, challenging racist practices.[55]

§3.8. AN INTEGRAL PART OF THE ETHOS

Recall the view Dewey put forward in the debate with Fry: the stock of "inner material" developed in the past (including "meanings and values," 1934, LW 10:95) is remade in creative activity. *Art as Experience* makes a related point—this time, in the social context. We give shape and meaning to our lives as we communicate with others: "the conveyance of meaning gives body and definiteness to the experience of the one who utters as well as to that of those who listen" (1934, LW 10:248–49). *Democracy and Education* echoes this. Communication helps us elaborate on the significance of our individual and collective experience: "A man really living alone (alone mentally as well as physically) would have little or no occasion to reflect upon his past experience to extract its net meaning" (1916, MW 9:8–9). We need a social context, a language, and an occasion to articulate the sense of our lives.

The abstract painter's search for fresh means to render the beauty of lines and colors on her canvas involves personal growth. So do our attempts to fashion the vocabularies and narratives that make sense of our experience. The effort "enlarges and enlightens experience; it stimulates and enriches imagination; it creates responsibility for accuracy and vividness of statement and thought" (1916, MW 9:8–9). We develop imagination, communicative skills, and sympathy. We elaborate on the meanings and values of our existence. This sort of growth isn't confined to artists. Ordinary human beings can do this, too, when they make an effort to communicate and listen. The rigid line between the fine arts and the arts of daily living disappears in Dewey's works: "the literary arts . . . are the enhanced continuations of social converse" (1925, LW 1:322). Art, as all genuine communication, breaks the barriers between us:

> Expression strikes below the barriers that separate human beings from one another. . . . Art . . . is the most universal and freest form of communication. Every intense experience of friendship and affection completes itself artistically. The sense of communion generated by a work of art may take on a definitely religious

quality. The union of men with one another is the source of the rites that from the time of archaic man to the present have commemorated the crises of birth, death, and marriage. Art is the extension of the power of rites and ceremonies to unite men, through a shared celebration, to all incidents and scenes of life. (1934, LW 10:275)

The passage gestures toward the political significance of the arts. They aren't mere useless luxuries in a social context. They help unite human beings across the barriers that divide them.[56]

This forms part of Dewey's larger analysis of the role of art in the development of culture. Recall the twofold nature of Dewey's project in *Art as Experience* laid out at the beginning of this chapter. One task is to explore the connection of aesthetic experience to personal growth. Another task is to explain how the arts contribute to communal development.

Here, too, Dewey appealed to Plato as a predecessor. He didn't read Plato as a simple-minded foe of the arts. Instead, Dewey saw him as paying tribute to their extraordinary power: "Plato's demand of censorship of poetry and music is a tribute to the social and even political influence exercised by those arts" (1934, LW 10:331). Dewey respected Plato for having recognized art's potential to shape individuals and communities. In ancient Athens, art "reflected the emotions and ideas that are associated with the chief institutions of social life . . . music was an integral part of the ethos and the institutions of the community. The idea of 'art for art's sake' would not have been even understood" (1934, LW 10:13).

The American pragmatist was clearly inspired by the role that the arts had once played in ancient Athens. *Art as Experience* laments the distancing of the arts from the life of modern societies (1934, LW 10:15). We're also told that the arts are "marvelous aids in the creation of . . . [a unified] life" in a community (1934, LW 10:87). The book celebrates "community of experience." Some passages even go so far as to criticize artists who "exaggerate their separateness to the point of eccentricity," giving their work "the air of something independent and esoteric" (1934, LW 10:15).

These passages are troubling. Was Dewey too harsh a critic of what he called "aesthetic individualism" (1934, LW 10:15)? Was his vision of communal unity facilitated by the arts potentially oppressive to individuals, especially those who criticize the ethos of their communities? Dewey tells us that in Athens, "Athletic sports, as well as drama, celebrated and *enforced* traditions of race and group, instructing the people, commemorating glories, and strengthening their civic pride" (1934, LW 10:13, my emphasis). He doesn't tell us that this is exactly the role he envisages for the arts in modern societies. But neither does he explicitly condemn the practice. The reference to "enforcing" the traditions of a particular group conjures up worrisome images of an unchallengeable monolithic ideology. We are reminded of art's role in the Simple Platonist's utopia: imaginative storytelling would be used to perpetuate a noble lie designed to keep the "masses" in their place. What would Dewey reply?

§3.9. THE BIRD IN OUR HANDS

Although Dewey wasn't particularly careful in the passages I just quoted, he was far from endorsing using the arts to enforce a single ideology. This goes against some of his most fundamental commitments. A charitable reading reveals several ways to mitigate the worry.

Dewey often emphasized the importance of inclusion and diversity in democratic dialogue. He lamented their absence: "because communication and participation are limited, sectarian, provincial, confined to class, party, professional group . . . our enjoyment of ends is luxurious and corrupting for some; brutal, trivial, harsh for others; exclusion from the life of free and full communication excluding both alike from full possession of meanings of the things that enter experience" (1925, LW 1:160). In his ideal community, art wouldn't serve to narrow down our horizons by enforcing a single group's worldview. Instead, it would widen our perspective as we engage with the lives and viewpoints of others. (We have already seen that Dewey celebrated art's ability to do this.) The unity created by art wouldn't be the result of erecting barriers through exclusion, prejudice, hatred, mistrust. It would be the result of breaking down such barriers. Of "reconstructing" the schemes through which we see the world and each other. Of challenging familiar narratives. And when, in this process, we find unanticipated points of contact with the lives of others, the emerging sense of "unity" is to be celebrated.

Art as Experience tells us that "[art] enables us to share vividly and deeply in meanings to which we had been dumb. . . . Communication is the process of creating participation, of making common what had been isolated and singular" (1934, LW 10:248–49). *Experience and Nature* echoes this point: "the fruit of communication . . . [is] participation, sharing" (1925, LW 1:132). Given his central commitments, Dewey should have added a qualification here. This "participation" shouldn't be enforced. It should emerge as we extend our sympathy and imagination, as we remake our habits of perception and action, as we attend to the lives of others.

Toni Morrison's Nobel Lecture captures this beautifully.[57] Part narrative and part reflection, it is itself a work of art. The lecture both *articulates* and *embodies* Morrison's vision of the power of literature to transform the way we live together. Morrison rejects the sort of language that serves a single ideology: "The conventional wisdom of the Tower of Babel story is that . . . one monolithic language would have expedited the building and heaven would have been reached. Whose heaven, she wonders? And what kind?" She celebrates the power of "vital" language to help us see each other afresh and shape new narratives. The live language of literature—"the bird in our hands"— can help us break through the bonds of oppressive communicative practices, challenging racist and sexist narratives:

> Oppressive language does more than represent violence; it is violence; does more than represent the limits of knowledge; it limits knowledge. Whether it is obscuring state language or the faux-language of mindless media; whether it is the proud but calcified language of the academy or the commodity driven language of science; whether it is the malign language of law-without-ethics, or language designed for the estrangement of minorities, hiding its racist plunder in its literary cheek—it must be rejected, altered and exposed. . . . Sexist language, racist language, theistic language—all are typical of the policing languages of mastery, and cannot, do not permit new knowledge or encourage the mutual exchange of ideas.

Though her analysis of oppressive language is far more sophisticated than was Dewey's, it resonates with his central moral concerns. He distinguished between communication and communities that are "vital" and those "cast in a mold," "routine" (1916,

MW 9:8–9). Our relationships, he worried, often remain on a "machine-like plane"; our exchanges reduced to the "giving and taking of orders," "without reference to the emotional or intellectual disposition and consent of those used" (1916, MW 9:8). Communication in modern societies is often subject to "oppressions, suppressions," "prejudice," "ignorance." Dewey clearly recognized that human beings can be seriously confined by defective communicative practices. He sought a radically different way of living together. Genuine democracy is a community where "communication is progressively liberated from bondage to prejudice and ignorance." This is what makes a thriving democratic culture educative: "the process of living together, when it is emancipated from oppressions and suppressions, becomes . . . a constant growth of that kind of understanding of our relations to one another that expels fear, suspicion and distrust" (1950, LW 17:86).

How can art help us build such communities?[58] Morrison doesn't just tell us—in her Nobel Lecture, she shows us that "narrative is radical, creating us at the very moment it is being created." Her lecture begins with a short parable. An old woman, "blind," "wise," "the daughter of slaves, black, American" lives alone on the city's outskirts. One day, she's visited by a group of children. Their purpose appears clear—they're "bent on disproving her clairvoyance." The children seem to mock the old woman when they ask whether the bird in their hands is alive or dead. She fails to answer. They can barely hold their laughter. Finally, she tells them she doesn't know whether the bird is alive or dead, "but what I do know is that it is in your hands." The old woman's response sounds like a subtle reprimand for "parading their power and her helplessness." The moral of the story seems obvious. And yet it isn't.

For the next half hour, Morrison interrogates the short parable, progressively dismantling all our assumptions about its characters and their motives. We learn that the children weren't trying to mock the old woman, after all. They merely wanted her attention and help. In Morrison's marvelous alternative ending, the children finally find a voice of their own:

> Why didn't you reach out, touch us with your soft fingers, delay the sound bite, the lesson, until you knew who we were? . . . You trivialize us and trivialize the bird that is not in our hands. Is there no context for our lives? No song, no literature, no poem full of vitamins, no history connected to experience that you can pass along to help us start strong? . . . Tell us about ships turned away from shorelines at Easter, placenta in a field. Tell us about a wagonload of slaves, how they sang so softly their breath was indistinguishable from the falling snow. How they knew from the hunch of the nearest shoulder that the next stop would be their last. How, with hands prayered in their sex, they thought of heat, then sun. Lifting their faces as though it was there for the taking. Turning as though there for the taking. They stop at an inn. The driver and his mate go in with the lamp leaving them humming in the dark. The horse's void steams into the snow beneath its hooves and its hiss and melt are the envy of the freezing slaves.

Morrison doesn't just tell us about the power of "vital" language to illuminate and shape our lives. We are shown its magic when the children speak. By building up and then subverting our expectations, the novelist makes it clear how easy it is for us to see each other through the prism of preconceptions. Her story shows how we can overcome them in a creative, sympathetic, imaginative dialogue. As audience, we're implicated in the conversation, invited to take part in the progressive reconstruction of the story. The old woman's blindness gains a different meaning when the children challenge her. But her closing remark offers yet another layer of complexity—she may have wanted to provoke them all along. "'Finally,' she says, 'I trust you now. I trust you with the bird that is not in your hands because you have truly caught it. Look. How lovely it is, this thing we have done—together.'"

§3.10. THE CLIMATE OF IMAGINATION

We can also mitigate the worry about art's unifying role by taking a closer look at Dewey's view on cultivating individuality. *Experience and Nature* tells us that expressing one's "irreducible uniqueness" may contribute to social development (1925, LW 1:188). Individuals shouldn't just conform to the status quo. Through their creative efforts, they can "reshape the world," introducing "innovations and deviations" (1925, LW 1:188). The arts help us remake the fabric of our shared experience. The view is echoed in *Art as Experience*:

> The material out of which a work of art is composed belongs to the common world rather than to the self, and yet there is self-expression in art because the self assimilates that material in a distinctive way to reissue it into the public world in a form that builds a new object. *This new object may have as its consequence similar reconstructions, recreations, of old and common material on the part of those who perceive it, and thus in time come to be established as part of the acknowledged world*—as "universal." (1934, LW 10:112–13, my emphasis)

Although she is creating something unique, the artist works with—and reshapes—material that is part of a world she shares with others. This might involve making changes in the physical environment (for instance, putting together paint and canvas to create a new object that others can enjoy). It might also involve more intangible changes. As we have already seen, Dewey thought that artists help remake our vocabularies, narratives, and ways of seeing one another (1934, LW 10:59).

We're starting to glimpse how the arts might simultaneously enable both personal growth and social development. A further detail can be added. They help us imagine new possibilities:

> Only imaginative vision elicits the possibilities that are interwoven within the texture of the actual. *The first stirrings of dissatisfaction and the first intimations of a better future are always found in works of art.* The impregnation of the characteristically new art of a period with *a sense of different values than those that prevail* is the reason why the conservative finds such art to be immoral and sordid, and is the reason why he resorts to the products of the past for esthetic satisfaction. (1934, LW 10:348, my emphases)

Experience and Nature tells us that the arts reshape the world through "innovations and deviations" (1925, LW 1:188). *Art as Experience* adds that the arts may express dissatisfaction with the status quo, articulate new values and imagine "a better future." They bring changes in "the climate of imagination" (1934, LW 10:348). The passage makes it clear that, in a Deweyan democracy, the arts wouldn't serve as means of enforcing a static ideology. They would help democratic citizens explore problems and imagine new solutions.

Dewey believed that we should figure out how to live in an open-ended, free, sympathetic, wide-ranging, imaginative conversation with other human beings. Among other things, this means engaging with voices that articulate neglected perspectives, express dissatisfaction with the existing state of affairs and offer visions of alternative ways of living. The arts (as "the enhanced continuations of social converse," 1925, LW 1:322) can become an important part of this sort of dialogue.

The proper role of the arts isn't to enforce a preset ideology. It is (at least partly) experimental. In this regard, Dewey even compares the artist to the scientist:

> There is, on the other side, a tendency among lay critics to confine experimentation to scientists in the laboratory. Yet one of the essential traits of the artist is that he is born an experimenter. Without this trait he becomes a poor or a good academician. . . . Only because the artist operates experimentally does he open new fields of experience and disclose new aspects and qualities in familiar scenes and objects. (1934, LW 10:148–49)

What does experimentation in the arts involve? Obviously, it might involve trying out different styles, shedding light on unconventional subjects, working in new media. But the range of the artist's experimentation doesn't end there. She might also explore different ways of living.[59] For instance, Tolstoy's fiction offers us a chance to examine different possibilities as we follow the fate of its myriad characters. Dewey admired and even quoted the novelist:

> We are accustomed," he [Tolstoy] says, "to consider moral doctrine as an insipid and monotonous affair, *in which there can be nothing new*. In reality human life with all its complicated and varied actions—*even those that seem to have nothing to do with*

morals, political activity, endeavor in the sciences, *the arts*, commerce—has no other object than to elucidate moral truths more and more. (ca. 1910–11, LW 17:389–90, my emphases)[60]

Given Dewey's emphasis on human development, it isn't surprising that this pragmatist thought the passage worth quoting. Tolstoy denies that "there can be nothing new" in the ethical realm. All human activities have a bearing on "elucidating" how we should live, the arts among them. From a Deweyan perspective, *War and Peace* offers us an imaginative vision of human possibilities, inviting us to reflect on whether its characters lead worthwhile lives. This connects to the account of moral deliberation found in *Human Nature and Conduct*. Dewey tells us that deliberation is experimental. It relies on our ability to imagine competing alternatives in a vivid way: "deliberation is a dramatic rehearsal (in imagination) of various competing possible lines of action. . . . It is an experiment in making various combinations of selected elements of habits and impulses, to see what the resultant action would be like if it were entered upon. *But the trial is in imagination*" (1992, MW 14:132, my emphasis). Dewey thinks that we respond to such imagined alternatives *just as if they were real*, "precisely as we would to the same objects if they were physically present" (1922, MW:139). Our capacity to imagine them so vividly is what allows us to try out different courses of action without actually having to pursue them. As we experiment with different alternatives in imagination, we figure out how we should live. Even if it is performed only in imagination, this sort of experimentation helps us learn.[61]

In Dewey's ideal democracy, the arts would be "part of the significant life of an organized community" (1934, LW 10:13), as they had once been in Athens. But the foregoing discussion makes it clear that he didn't envisage the arts as enforcing a single monolithic ideology. Their role isn't just to *reflect* the ethos of a community. It is to help us *develop* that ethos.

Recall the view of Deweyan democracy reconstructed in chapter 2. This form of life requires that we develop and exercise the kind of creativity, sympathy, and imagination he associated with the arts. Dewey's political philosophy and his aesthetics are connected. Both emphasize creativity and growth. Taking education seriously helps Dewey reorient both fields. By focusing on how art enables human development, individual and communal, Dewey also sheds light on art's political significance.[62] The rigid demarcation between the two fields disappears in his works.

§3.11. THE COMMON PATTERN OF ART?

Now we can add even more detail to our portrait of the great American pragmatist. As a philosopher of education, Dewey wasn't just a kindly kindergarten reformer. In his works, education served as "the supreme human interest" (1930, LW 5:156) guiding philosophical reflection. His aesthetics was no exception. Focusing on growth helped Dewey reorient the field away from "esoteric" debates—towards a naturalistic, pragmatic understanding of art. His novel project explored how art fosters personal growth and communal development.

The new program advocated by Dewey is promising. But it isn't unproblematic. One issue is his emphasis on what he calls "the consummatory phase" of growth. We are told that when equilibrium is regained after disruption in the process of growth, there is "consummation akin to the aesthetic" (1934, LW 10:20). It isn't entirely clear how exactly this phase should be defined and what good examples of it might look like. Sometimes, there is no clear completion, satisfaction, or resolution of tension in aesthetic experience.[63] This is captured beautifully in Musil's reflections on Rilke: "I called this impression [of Rilke's poetry] . . . a clear stillness in a never-pausing movement, a daring presumption, an elevated enduring, a broad openness, an almost painful tension. And one might well add that tensions most easily take on the character of pain when they cannot be entirely understood or resolved, when they form a knot in the discharge of our feelings."[64]

The power of Rilke's poetry lies in its ability to sustain unresolved tension. Earlier in the piece, Musil points out that "In the realm of the aesthetic . . . even imperfection and lack of completion have their value." From this perspective, Dewey's emphasis on "consummation" appears too narrow. It may obscure what's particularly moving, even revelatory, about some aesthetic experiences: their ability to create and sustain a "painful tension," allowing us to explore "knots in the discharge of our feelings" without providing a clear resolution.[65]

This brings me to another issue. *Art as Experience* claims that artistic, creative activities help "unify" our characters: "it is the office of art in the individual person, to compose differences, to do away with isolations and conflicts among the elements of our being, to utilize oppositions among them to build a richer personality" (1934, LW 10:252–53). But he never tells us why this is desirable. Nor does he tell us what such characters would look like. Do all inner conflicts have to be resolved? Can persistent, unsolved tensions be enriching? Here, too, we find echoes of Dewey's lifelong obsession with wholeness. Dewey's aesthetics was marked by his peculiar "demand for unification" that "was doubtless an intense emotional craving" (1930, LW 5:153), as the pragmatist himself acknowledged.

Dewey advocated cultivating "well-rounded" personalities (1934, LW 10:252) as an antidote to the plight of specialization. The worry might then be rephrased: Was Dewey too dismissive of specialists? Aren't there fields in which specialization might still be enriching? Perhaps Dewey was interested in "unification" understood as overcoming oppositions between what we ordinarily call "reason" and "emotion," "intellect" and "sentiment," "body" and "soul." In art and creative activity, "the whole creature is alive" (1934, LW 10:33) in a manner that makes it inappropriate to make such distinctions. Taking this interpretive route makes sense in light of Dewey's insistence that we let go of what he calls "compartmentalized psychology" when we think about art (1934, LW 10:253). But this, too, raises a further question: How exactly does this sort of unification aid the development of personality? Dewey doesn't provide a clear answer.[66]

My final worry is whether Dewey overemphasized growth. Do some aesthetic experiences resonate more with (or rest more on) already existing habits? How radical does the reconstruction of habits have to be at each stage? Dewey gave no clear answers there, either. He wanted to ground his aesthetics in a broader account of the overarching rhythms of life and nature—"the basic pattern of the relations of the live creature to his environment" (1934, LW 10:155). As he saw it, this constitutes "the common pattern of art" (1934, LW 10:155). On this view, the rhythms of disruption and adjustment, of tension and consummation in the processes of growth are fundamental to all sorts of experience. But the effort to subsume a vast variety of aesthetic experiences under one pattern—"the common pattern of art" (1934, LW 10:155)—may obscure significant differences.

Michele Moody-Adams's work illuminates an important function of the arts that doesn't seem to fit within the Deweyan framework: their ability to offer consolation (by reminding us that grief, sorrow, and suffering are a fundamental part of life). Artworks that help us appreciate the inevitability of suffering don't seem to be "consummatory" in the sense that Dewey attached to the term. Perhaps he could reply that such artworks lead to growth as we develop our capacity to appreciate and face the emotional complexity and inherent sorrow of human experience. But Dewey never discussed these types of aesthetic experiences. His optimistic temper seems to have blinded him to these important functions of art. Dewey's effort to subsume all aesthetic experience under one "common pattern" may obscure significant variations in how the arts function. As Moody-Adams's work shows, the arts may contribute to our well-being in a variety of ways: transformation, reconciliation, and consolation.[67]

He often criticized philosophers for trying to impose one pattern on life. The charge could be levied against him, too. There was something almost Platonic in the zeal with which Dewey invoked the pattern of growth in every context. Aesthetic experience is probably a lot more varied and complex than he recognized. Perhaps "aesthetic experience" is a loosely connected family of experiences, not all of which fit squarely into the disruption-adjustment-consummation framework.

Even by his own standards, Dewey's aesthetics is incomplete. One of his best insights was that we should pay closer attention to the place of aesthetic experience in the overall life history of each individual. This means that providing a full account of aesthetic experience requires a lot more than describing "the common pattern of art." We need to pay more attention to individual variations than did Dewey. And we need better knowledge of human psychology than was available in his day. *Art as Experience* is only a starting point.

Taking art's growth-enabling power seriously calls for exploring the varieties of aesthetic experience by engaging more with
concrete individuals and specific works of art. (See, for instance,
Philip Kitcher's reflections on *Death in Venice*.) We also need
more in-depth studies of how the arts help cultures develop at
various historical junctures. See, for example, Robert Gooding-
Williams's analysis of how Du Bois's *Jesus Christ in Texas* challenges racial oppression; see, too, Moody-Adams's analysis of the
role that the art of civic remembrance has played in enhancing
American democracy and challenging racial injustice. The project can also be continued by disputing the strict divide between
the fine and popular arts, as does Richard Shusterman when he
examines the aesthetic qualities of rap music.[68]

We needn't think all art performs (or must perform) just the
functions Dewey emphasized. But we can still value his aesthetics for pointing out some of the ways in which art can help us
grow and thrive. We can still learn from the seriousness with
which he took art and creativity in education and in public life.
For this American pragmatist, reflecting on aesthetics wasn't just
an "esoteric" pursuit of interest to a few specialists. It was an
important part of a larger inquiry into human development and
flourishing. One of the most unique features of Dewey's aesthetics was how it challenged the separation between "high" aesthetic pleasures and the aesthetics of ordinary life. The daily
existence of the "mass" isn't essentially and unavoidably unaesthetic. Reforms in education, changes in socioeconomic institutions, even conceptual revisions in aesthetic theory can help
enhance the richness of experience for the "mass" of human
beings, whom modernist "esoteric" theorists confined forever to
"kitsch."[69]

Equally significant was Dewey's attempt to erase the
hard-and-fast distinction between art as a means of individual

self-expression and art as a means of developing the community's ethos. The artist's vision is often in tension with the norms of society. But this doesn't relegate art to irrelevance. It doesn't doom the artist to eternal solitude. A quintessential optimist, Dewey believed in the power of art to overcome barriers, estrangement, and confinement, transforming our communities. What about artists who explicitly embrace solitude, disavowing their ties to others? For instance, the young Rilke wrote in his *Diaries* of art as a solitary enterprise. Still, Rilke's poetry has the communicative power Dewey celebrated. Particularly useful here is the pragmatist's distinction between the intent and the consequence of the artist's work: "I do not say that communication to others is the intent of the artist. But it is the consequence of his work—which indeed lives only in communication when it operates in the experience of others." Nor did Dewey equate communicability with popularity: "Indifference to response of the immediate audience is a necessary trait of all artists that have something new to say. But they are animated by a deep conviction that since they can only say what they have to say, the trouble is not with their work by those who, having eyes, see not, and having ears, hear not. Communicability has nothing to do with popularity" (1934, LW 10:110). Of course, there are probably works of art that fall well outside—and challenge—Dewey's "communicative" view of the arts. But the position is still valuable if it captures the growth-enabling effects of at least some artworks.

His vision presents a powerful challenge to those who think that art and aesthetic experience must be forever detached from common human concerns. It stands in stark contrast with the spirit of avant-garde art as articulated by Ortega y Gasset, who tells us that modern art seeks to "renounce its importance," dividing human beings into those who understand it and those who don't, "compelling the people to recognize itself for what it is: a component among others of the social structure, inert matter of the historical process, a secondary factor in the cosmos of spiritual life."[70] This couldn't have been further from Dewey's view.

Dewey's unfinished project is still relevant today. It gives us resources to resist narrow conceptions of utility that see the arts as "useless frills" in education and in public life. Those who dismiss the arts fail to appreciate their educative and growth-enabling potential. It also gives us resources to resist "esoteric" conceptions of art.[71] Elitist modernist critics were wrong to limit aesthetic experience to that of a few "artists" in circumstances remote from the rest of life. Art and aesthetic experience should once again be reconnected to the lives of ordinary human beings—in theory and in practice.

4

FLOURISHING AND EDUCATION

§4.1. TAKING EDUCATION SERIOUSLY

What would it mean to take philosophy of education seriously? Reading Dewey afresh reveals the answers. Philosophy of education isn't just a matter of considering how classrooms should be organized, what should be taught, how educational decisions are made, and so on. For Dewey, education was the proper orientation of philosophy itself. Taking education seriously means reorienting the discipline. It means placing questions about human development (and about the shape of human experience that emerges under the different arrangements, formal and informal, that educate us) at the center of our philosophical inquiries. As I have tried to show, education was much more than a mere side project in his vast philosophical oeuvre. In appreciating the importance of education to the discipline, Dewey belongs to a tradition of thought that includes Plato, Rousseau, and Du Bois, among others. (Here I focus on Dewey's explicit interlocutors—of course, this isn't an exhaustive list of thinkers, but only a starting point for outlining the tradition of philosophy of education.) We might view that tradition as yielding an "alternative canon" that focuses on human development.

Dewey once complained that he wasn't being criticized for his unorthodox approach to the discipline. Philosophers just ignored it: "philosophers in general . . . have not taken education with sufficient seriousness for it to occur to them that any rational person could actually think it possible that philosophizing should focus about education as the supreme human interest in which, moreover, other problems, cosmological, moral, logical, come to a head" (1930, LW 5:156). To be sure, there are plenty of books on Dewey. Still, none shows how education served as "the supreme human interest" at the heart of Dewey's oeuvre.[1] One of his most provocative ideas—an unorthodox conception of philosophy that anchors a vast array of inquiries in an overarching interest in human development—hasn't been fully appreciated.

I have tried to present a fresh portrait of Dewey as an educational theorist. Although Dewey's critique of early twentieth-century schooling in *Democracy and Education* deserves its fame, his philosophy of education was an even more ambitious undertaking. It involved formulating a general theory of human development (or growth) and criticizing practices and habits in many spheres of life—from daily life in democracies to museum art—that affect human development.[2] Thinking about formal schooling was part of that enormous enterprise. Like Plato, Rousseau, and Du Bois, Dewey didn't think that the training of the young is too "soft" a topic for serious philosophers.[3] But he also recognized that education doesn't end when we leave school. It isn't confined to formal settings. We're educated by living together. We're transformed by the arts. We're shaped by our socioeconomic institutions. To understand how we become who we are and how we might do better at furthering our individual and communal development "under the influences of associated life" (1920, MW 12:193) has a profound bearing on human flourishing.

"What sort of individuals are created?" (1920, MW 12:193) How do various habits, institutions, concepts in every sphere of "associated life" shape human beings? How can we improve those arrangements in order to facilitate human development? How can we educate human beings so that they may enjoy richer experiences and continue improving the practices that affect them and their fellows?[4] Dewey conceived of such questions as central to the philosophy of the future.

And Dewey practiced what he preached. I have attempted to make it clear that education is indeed "the supreme human interest" (1930, LW 5:156) guiding his philosophical reflections on democracy and art. These two Deweyan examples, explored in chapters 2 and 3, reveal how we might do philosophy in a way that places education at the center.

Education becomes a focal point for Dewey's political theory when he reconceptualizes democracy not just as a set of institutions, but as a personal way of life that has character-shaping effects. A thriving democratic culture enlarges the sensibility, sympathy, and intelligence of those who take part in it. It might even allow entire communities to grow as they reflect on their values, goals, and ways of living together. This is education *by* democracy. Education *for* democracy is equally important, and it goes far beyond teaching "civics." To foster a flourishing democratic ethos, schooling should promote growth-enabling habits (such as sympathy, creativity, and criticism) that allow the individual to contribute to the continual development of her community. By focusing on education, Dewey reorients political philosophy. In his works, reflecting on democracy is inseparable from thinking about character formation. Against all naysayers, Dewey tells us that the personalities of "democratic individuals" are flourishing and rich. His project—examining how democratic everyday practices might shape us and how we might, in turn, shape them—remains as relevant today as ever.

Focusing on education (understood as growth) helped Dewey reorient aesthetics away from "esoteric" (1934, LW 10:94) debates toward a naturalistic, pragmatic understanding of art. His novel project in *Art as Experience* explores how art fosters personal growth and communal development. (We're told, for instance, that art helps us appreciate hitherto hidden aspects of life and extend our sympathy to a wider range of specific human predicaments.) *Art as Experience* probes the relationship between aesthetic experience and personal growth. And it embeds art in a greater picture of human development, examining "its role in civilization" (1934, LW 10:16). In line with the large pragmatic program outlined in chapter 1, Dewey's unorthodox aesthetics also diagnoses the effects of removing the arts from the ordinary lives of the "mass" of human beings and from the life of the community as a whole (1934, LW 10:12–15).

By focusing on how art enables individual and communal development, Dewey also sheds light on art's political significance. The rigid distinction between political philosophy and aesthetics disappears in his works; two apparently distinct inquiries into democracy and into art can be linked by focusing on education.

We should also recall a further aspect of Dewey's program. He didn't just defend the substantive centrality of education to philosophy. He also argued for its methodological importance: "Education is the laboratory in which philosophic distinctions become concrete and are tested" (1916, MW 9:339). Philosophies shouldn't be developed and evaluated apart from how they influence the formation of our fundamental dispositions. Dewey's radical vision of philosophy as something that has to be tested in real life resonates with the perspective of William James. "The

Sentiment of Rationality" laments the tendency of philosophers to take all their problems as merely intellectual issues.[5] For these two pragmatists, the proper place of philosophical reflection is intermediary and hypothetical. We should test philosophies in action. Education can be a means to do this. Dewey's unorthodox "methodological centrality thesis" reminds us that education connects philosophy to the trial and error of life.

§4.2. THE SYSTEMATIC MEANS TO FLOURISHING

Dewey's unorthodox project fits into a broader tradition that takes philosophy of education seriously. Recall that education was *the* lens through which he viewed the history of philosophy. Seen through this lens, underappreciated aspects of the philosophical tradition come to light, revealing the contours of an "alternative canon" that focuses on education "in its largest sense." Understanding Dewey as I have proposed, standard pictures of the history of Western thought, whether they are centered on the careers of metaphysics, or of epistemology, or of ethics, ignore a different way of viewing philosophy's achievements.

In appreciating the centrality of education to the discipline, Dewey was inspired by the ancients, especially by Plato. In ancient Greece, he writes, "The educational enterprise was *taken seriously*. It was regarded as *the systematic means by which the good life was to be arrived at and maintained*: the life full, excellent, rich, for the individual centre of that life, and the life good for the community of which the individual was a member" (1929–30, LW 5:291, my emphases).

Like Plato, Dewey believed that taking philosophy of education seriously involves far more than thinking about how we might reform schooling to achieve some narrow, unexamined end, creating "sharps in learning" (1916, MW 9:12).[6] Education is "the systematic means" to furthering human flourishing. Philosophy of education "in its largest sense" involves examining and criticizing the institutions, practices, habits, conceptions that have a bearing on human development and imagining new possibilities. Like Plato's *Republic*, Dewey's *Democracy and Education* was an effort to take education seriously in this way. Although they disagreed on many things, both philosophers offered educational theories that were systematic perspectives of wide scope. For both Plato and Dewey, human development—or education—in accordance with a certain conception of flourishing forms an anchor for social critique and for imagining new possibilities. Both thinkers offer a vision of flourishing informed by a specific perspective on human psychology. For Plato, the good life is characterized by harmony of the whole, which is led by the best, rational, part of the soul. For Dewey, the good life is one of open-ended growth in community with others. Human development also connects different areas of philosophical inquiry (such as political theory and aesthetics).

Both believed that political arrangements shape and are in turn shaped by the characters of individual citizens. Dewey credited Plato with appreciating this: "It would be impossible to find in any scheme of philosophic thought a more adequate recognition on one hand of the educational significance of social arrangements and, on the other, of the dependence of those arrangements upon the means used to educate the young" (1916, MW 9:95). The weight Plato attached to the question of the education of the young in the *Republic* bears an affinity to the seriousness with which Dewey approached early twentieth-century schooling in America.[7] Plato's well-known critique of "the democratic character" and Dewey's impassioned defense of "the democratic individual" certainly seem to place them at odds. Where they agree, however, is in focusing their political philosophy on character formation. "What sort of individuals are created?" (1920, MW 12:193). The question Dewey posed toward the end of his passionate manifesto for "reconstructing philosophy" was also Plato's. The question looms large in the discussion of the different character types (and corresponding cities) in Book VIII of the *Republic*. Political arrangements are evaluated based on the type of individuals they help shape. And the examination of the ideal city's viability centers on how to educate its citizens. Education isn't just a side-topic. It's a focal point for political thought.

When it comes to aesthetics, Dewey and Plato seem utterly at odds. Socrates's well-known critique of the arts in the *Republic* could not be farther from Dewey's enthusiastic endorsement of art's enriching, growth-enabling power. Yet focusing exclusively on this disagreement obscures an intriguing affinity. Both thinkers took seriously the idea that the arts educate us. Both used the idea as an anchor for their respective aesthetic theories. Dewey even enlisted Plato as an ally in *Art as Experience* when he argued against "esoteric" theories of art that discount their human significance: "Plato felt this connection [between art and the institutions of social life] so strongly that it led him to his idea of the necessity of censorship of poets, dramatists, and musicians. Perhaps he exaggerated when he said that a change from the Doric to the Lydian mode in music would be the sure precursor of civic degeneration. But no contemporary would have doubted that music was an integral part of the ethos and the institutions of the community. The idea of 'art for art's sake' would not have been even understood" (1934, LW 10:13).

Plato recognized that art can shape individual characters and affect the ethos of entire communities. In fact, it was precisely because of the centrality of Homer to ancient Greek education and morals that Plato was so keen to dispute the poet's moral and educative authority in the *Republic*. Dewey understood this: "Plato's demand of censorship of poetry and music is a tribute to the social and even political influence exercised by those arts" (1934, LW 10:331). Crucially, for both thinkers, this influence is exercised via the formative power of the arts.[8] Of course, they disagreed on *how* the arts shape characters. They also disagreed on the extent to which the arts prepare us for a flourishing life: Plato's Socrates focuses on the educative effect of the arts to find fault with some of them (and to outline a program for "purifying" the arts). Dewey's appreciation of the educative effects of the arts pulls in a different direction—democratizing the arts, including a wider range of pursuits in the purview of the aesthetic, and embracing the creativity and growth they might further. Still, the formative value of the arts isn't just a side issue in aesthetics, either for Plato or for Dewey. It is central.

These affinities shouldn't obscure important differences. On Dewey's modern pragmatic view, philosophy of education is historically situated, rooted in the appreciation for the latest results of the natural sciences (including psychology and evolutionary biology), democratic and cooperative. Philosophical inquiry as Dewey conceived it is historically situated and open-ended: there is no absolutely perfect character (or absolutely perfect set of institutions) revealed by philosophy once and for all.[9] And there is no perfect education that would go along with this. Moreover, inquiry into human flourishing isn't the exclusive purview of the philosophical elite: "philosophy . . . has no private access to good. . . . It accepts the goods that are diffused in human experience. It has no Mosaic or Pauline authority of revelation entrusted to it. But it has the authority of intelligence, of criticism of these common and natural goods" (1925, LW 1:305, my emphasis).

In the ideal Deweyan democracy, every individual would have a chance to take part in a wider conversation, contributing to some extent to this enterprise. It is a "cooperative effort" (1929, LW 4:250), one in which philosophy is joined by the arts (including those of democratic "social converse") conducted by ordinary human beings (1925, LW 1:322). Taking education seriously, for Dewey, doesn't just involve doing philosophy of education understood narrowly as a specialized field. It also means engaging in a wider communal inquiry into human flourishing. This democratic conception of inquiry goes hand in hand with a humbler understanding of the philosopher's role. Dewey didn't see himself as providing fixed and final answers. He made provisional suggestions that contribute to (but don't seek to exhaust) this larger project.

Here we glimpse an interesting continuity between Dewey's overall conception of philosophy and his proposals for educational reform. Rejecting the idea that philosopher-kings should rule in favor of having a democratic conversation on the ends and goods of existence goes hand in hand with the idea that individuals should be educated to take part in that greater democratic conversation. Reflecting on how we might reform schooling to prepare human beings for this was, of course, the aim of Dewey's most famous book, *Democracy and Education*.[10]

If Dewey had such a wide-ranging conception of inquiry into human flourishing, why did he think that we should do *philosophy* of education at all? What can the discipline contribute? *Reconstruction in Philosophy* suggests that it has a double task: a "negative" task of criticism, as well as the more "positive" task of imagining new possibilities (1920, MW 12:155). *The Quest for Certainty* tells us that philosophy's "critical mind" should "be directed against the domination exercised by prejudice, narrow interest, routine custom" (1929, LW 4:248–49). This should be supplemented by "the creative work of the imagination in pointing to the new possibilities which knowledge of the actual discloses" (1929, LW 4:248–49). Dewey probably wasn't alone in thinking that philosophy of education has a negative task of criticism, as well as a positive task of imagining new possibilities and envisaging experiments.[11] Plato, Jean-Jacques Rousseau, and W. E. B. Du Bois might have agreed with this (after all, their works offer both criticism and imagination of new possibilities). But Dewey was unique in seeing the voice of philosophy as only one in a greater conversation that spans the whole community.

§4.3. THE MEASURE OF THE POSSIBLE

Rousseau would have agreed that philosophy of education should extend our imagination to appreciate a wider range of human options: "it is imagination that extends for us the measure of the possible." That is why his educational treatise *Emile* is a romantic novel. He is another interlocutor of Dewey's who can be included in an "alternative canon" that focuses on human development.

Like Dewey's *Democracy and Education*, Rousseau's *Emile* was an attempt to respond to the *Republic*, continuing the ancient inquiry in modern times. (Indeed, in *Emile*, Rousseau calls the *Republic* "the most beautiful educational treatise ever written.") At first sight, *Emile* might look more like a practical handbook for parents than a serious philosophical work, and Rousseau himself sometimes encourages this reading.[12] But a close reading reveals that this impression is misleading. Rousseau didn't think of philosophy of education as a narrow field of interest to teachers and parents alone. Like Dewey, Rousseau took education to be a fundamental issue for political philosophy.

One might interpret *Emile* as giving us Rousseau's vision of the education of the ideal citizen, without which his political writings would be radically incomplete. *Emile* invokes Plato as a predecessor who took public education seriously. As Rousseau sees it, the problems of his time demand renewing Plato's inquiry in the modern context. Unlike the ancient citizen who was ready to sacrifice private interest for the public good, the modern bourgeois is always torn between the two: "Always in contradiction with himself, always floating between his inclinations and his duties, he will never be either man or citizen. He will be good neither for himself nor for others. He will be one of these men of our days: a Frenchman, an Englishman, a bourgeois. He will be nothing."[13] Deceitful, inauthentic, conflicted, selfish, vain and dominating, the modern bourgeois is difficult material from which to fashion a good citizen. But Rousseau takes up the challenge: his answer is to avoid the development of these traits early on—to isolate Emile from all the influences that would otherwise make him into the bourgeois character Rousseau condemns. Strictly speaking, then, Rousseau isn't really molding the existing bourgeois into citizens, but imagining how citizen education might go when conducted completely from scratch and away from all the influences of the social life of his day. This task is all the more difficult because it involves harmonizing private happiness and public good. Rousseau doesn't just seek to cultivate a good citizen. He also wants to educate a flourishing human being who achieves private happiness in accordance with "nature." How can this kind of person be educated? Is it possible? Are there ineradicable obstacles that prevent the full realization of Rousseau's ideal?[14] Reflecting on these questions is an important task for those interested in political philosophy and ethics. Rousseau's attack on the thinness of the political philosophy of the Enlightenment *philosophes* (who disregarded the sentimental education of human beings at their own peril) resonates with Dewey's worries about a philosophy that has become enmeshed in technicalities at the expense of thinking about human development.

My reading of Rousseau suggests a vision of the centrality of education to political philosophy and ethics akin to Plato's and Dewey's perspective on the importance of the field. On this picture, education facilitates human flourishing, individual and communal (and seeks to harmonize the two). Another task of Rousseau's *Emile* is that of social critique—diagnosing current problems and trying to identify their root causes. Analyzing the destructive psychological effects of socialization in modern bourgeois societies inspired some of Rousseau's most provocative and impassioned writing. Recall the opening pages of *Emile*, where he charges modern civilization with creating "deformity, monsters": "All our wisdom consists in servile prejudices. All our practices are only subjection, impediment, and constraint. Civil man is born, lives, and dies in slavery. At his birth he is sewed in swaddling clothes; at his death he is nailed in a coffin. So long as he keeps his human shape, he is enchained by our institutions . . . I do not see what he gained by being born." This polemic eventually gives way to a more detailed analysis of how specific educational practices "deform" human beings. He believed, for instance, that the way adults react to tears may condition children to seek to manipulate and dominate others. More generally, Rousseau worried that the natural (and, to his mind, harmless, if properly managed) human drive of self-love turns into vanity under the influence of defective education and socialization.[15] That inflamed vanity, together with social arrangements that engender mutual dependence, creates destructive personal and social consequences. On the personal side, it creates inauthentic individuals torn apart by conflicting impulses. On the social side, it fuels tyranny and inequality. Much like Plato's and Dewey's, Rousseau's philosophy of education encompasses psychological analysis and social critique. Social arrangements are miseducative. This is why Emile has to be removed far from society to be educated in private by the ideal tutor: in a striking passage at the beginning of *Emile*, Rousseau likens the child to a "nascent shrub away from the highway" around which one must build a "fence."[16] Showing that social arrangements are miseducative is also showing that they are bad. They create human beings who fall short of their true potential (for Rousseau, living freely, in accordance with "nature" and in harmony with other human beings). It also involves formulating a conception of human flourishing with which the criticized arrangements conflict.

Reading Rousseau carefully reveals that education can be a focal point for social critique. The miseducative quality of social arrangements can be one of the reasons to condemn them. Here, once again, we see resonances with Plato and Dewey. Of course, they thought of the miseducative effects of the reigning social arrangements (and of the proper remedies) in ways that differed widely. On the Platonic view, they are miseducative to the extent that they encourage the "lower" parts of the soul (such as desire for money and recognition) to rule. Plato was worried that the educative practices, customs, and institutions of his day led even the best citizens astray. The most talented Athenians spent their time chasing riches and social status. They left philosophy "desolate and unwed" while "they themselves lead lives that are inappropriate and untrue." Good education would rescue the best part of human nature from these pernicious influences (in which "the best nature . . . is destroyed and corrupted, so that it cannot follow the best way of life") for the sake of realizing full human potential (in the few who have the "rare" gift).[17]

Dewey's approach, of course, was different. When he worried about the miseducative effects of the reigning social arrangements and practices, he focused on issues such as the plight of the factory worker under industrial capitalism (his reflections on this resonate with Marx).[18] Many human beings are forced to live lives devoid of opportunities to develop their capacities, to enjoy rich aesthetic experiences, to pursue creative, fulfilling jobs. Routine, dullness, blind adherence to authority and custom, barriers to inclusion in activities and opportunities that would help one realize one's full potential and enjoy fulfilling experiences— these were the issues close to Dewey's heart. The reigning social arrangements are miseducative to the extent that they prevent all human beings, irrespective of their background, to access growth-enabling opportunities and to enjoy a "life worth living" (1920, MW 12:200–201) in community with others. It was with such concerns in mind that Dewey argued that "the moral meaning of democracy" is to give all human beings equal opportunity to develop their capacities "without respect to race, sex, class or economic status" (1920, MW 12:186; see also 1939, LW 14:226).

§4.4. CONTRARY TO HUMAN NATURE?

Rousseau's *Emile* also illustrates the potential pitfalls of philosophy of education. I am referring to his views on women's education. Emile's future wife, Sophie, is educated for a life of confining domesticity and obedience. To make matters worse, her training stands in striking contrast with Emile's preparation for independence and freedom. She isn't even allowed to study philosophy and science. She is expected to take all her views on these subjects from Emile. All the while, Emile is taught to stop relying on the authority of others. Already in the opening pages of the chapter on Sophie's education, this sexist approach is made clear: "Sophie ought to be a woman . . . she ought to have everything which suits the constitution of her species and her sex *to fill her place* in the physical and moral order." Rousseau takes himself to be describing education adapted to "women's nature." Ironically, the program is irrevocably marred by the conventions and gender biases of his time. For a thinker who claims to be rejecting all convention in favor of recovering an "original human nature," not "deformed" by civilization, this is a particularly strong indictment. Rousseau's resounding failure when it comes to reflecting on women's education casts a shadow over *Emile*.[19] The gender biases that so deeply mar Rousseau's conception of the "education of nature" reveal the pitfalls of making grand claims about "human nature" based on unexamined prejudice. Worse still, Rousseau explicitly rejected the claims of women to being treated equally with men by arguing that it is contrary to "nature," which is the expression of the will of God.[20]

Dewey recognized this danger. His theory of education is remarkable for resisting appeals to a fixed "human nature." Conceptions of a fixed and apparently readily observable "human nature," he knew, can be used to resist necessary change:

> In the past, changes in institutions, that is in fundamental customs, have been opposed on the ground that they were contrary to Nature in its most universal sense, and hence to the will and reason of God as the Founder of Nature. One has only to go back to the arguments advanced against the abolition of human slavery to see that such was the case. More recently still, many opponents of the idea of enfranchising women used the argument that

it was contrary to the very laws of Nature and of Nature's God. Such facts prove how strong is the tendency to use well-established habits as the proper standard and measure of what is natural and unnatural (1940, LW 14:259).

The passage doesn't explicitly engage with Rousseau, but the critique resonates deeply with the concerns I just raised. Rousseau rejected gender equality in just the terms Dewey described. This couldn't have been further from Dewey's stance. By contrast to those who would narrowly circumscribe human possibilities based on their belonging to a certain group (classifying them by class, gender or race), Dewey dreamed of giving opportunities for having the richest possible experience and education to all human beings. We can connect Dewey's rejection of appeals to fixed human nature in "Contrary to Human Nature" to his condemnation of racial and gender prejudice in "Racial Prejudice and Friction" (1922, MW 13:248). The moral meaning of democracy is to give equal opportunity for development to all human beings, "without respect to race, sex, class or economic status" (1920, MW 12:186; see also 1939, LW 14:226). This commitment was central to the moral vision motivating his work on democracy and on education.

Dewey didn't think human beings belong to predefined social classes or types. Nor did he think it possible to tell exactly what human beings are capable of until they have been given access to the right kinds of educational opportunities. In response to skepticism about his faith in democratic schooling, Dewey insisted that we don't know the extent of human potential until we have "tried the educational experiment" (1922, MW 13:293). He believed that faulty institutions are complicit in fostering "mediocrity." They are miseducative. That is precisely why he condemned them.

§4.5. THE PROBLEM OF PROBLEMS

The seriousness with which Du Bois took philosophy of education is captured in "The Immortal Child": "All human problems, then, center in the immortal Child and *his education is the problem of problems*."[21] Du Bois took education seriously as one of the central issues for a philosophy that aims at facilitating social progress. How might education help dismantle structures of racial oppression? What are some of the pitfalls of education under racial oppression? What is the value—and what should be the shape—of liberal education in this context? These questions loom large in his college addresses, collected in *The Education of Black People*. They are also explored in *The Souls of Black Folk* and the autobiographical *Darkwater*, a chapter of which, "The Immortal Child," eloquently argues in favor of overcoming barriers to human flourishing and development erected by racism. Du Bois saw education as "the creator of . . . freedom and equality."[22] He condemned the educational institutions of his time for maintaining the status quo, instead of facilitating social progress and opening up opportunities for flourishing to all human beings, irrespective of their race: "the majority of the children of the world are not being systematically fitted for their life work and *for life itself*. . . . That failure is due to the fact that we aim not at the full development of the child, but that the world regards and always has regarded education first as a means of buttressing the established order of things rather than improving it."[23]

The reference to "life itself" suggests a broad conception of education that goes far beyond mere "technical," "vocational" training. Du Bois bears an affinity to the other thinkers considered here in taking education seriously as a means to furthering the flourishing of well-rounded human beings. Its proper end is enriching "life itself." As Du Bois saw it, at its best education can become a means of liberating human capacities and of inspiring African American students to fight for social justice.[24] His expansive vision of a flourishing, well-rounded life is captured in one of his addresses at Fisk:

> What then is Life—What is it for—What is its great End? Manifestly in the light of all knowledge, and according to the testimony of all men who have lived, *life is the fullest, most complete enjoyment of the possibilities of human existence.* It is the development and broadening of the feelings and emotions, through sound and color, line and form. It is technical mastery of the media that these paths and emotions need for expression of their full meaning. It is the free enjoyment of every normal appetite. It is giving rein to the creative impulse. . . . Here roots the rise of the Joy of Living, of music, painting, drawing, sculpture and building; hence comes literature with romance, poetry and essay; hence rise Love, Friendship, emulation, and ambition, and the ever widening realms of thought, in increasing circles of apprehended and interpreted Truth.[25]

Du Bois's conception of genuine life is heavily centered on what we might think of as artistic issues, such as creativity and self-expression. The "most complete enjoyment of the possibilities of human existence" involves having opportunities to develop one's emotions and means of expression. It requires the kind of creative freedom an artist might enjoy. All this is underscored by another striking suggestion: "living in the fuller and broader sense of the term is the expression of art."[26] Du Bois saw the creativity, freedom, and richness of emotions and meanings associated with artistic activity as central to a worthwhile life. Education shouldn't shun the task of preparing human beings, irrespective of their background, for living in this "fuller and broader sense."

Du Bois's writings examine how racism limits opportunities for this sort of education. They also investigate the specific pitfalls—and the promise—of education for social progress. This theme is prominent in "Of the Coming of John," in *The Souls of Black Folk*, where Du Bois explores how education might (or might not) enhance one's ability to resist and dismantle racist practices. "Of the Coming of John" also illuminates tragic tensions between certain forms of personal development and communal belonging.[27] Du Bois went much further than Dewey ever did in probing education under racial oppression. Still, the two thinkers can be seen as allies in seeking to facilitate "a life worth living" for all human beings through education.[28]

Earlier I outlined the most general questions of a philosophy that focuses on education. How do the current social arrangements educate us? How can we improve them? How can we educate human beings to take a part in improving them? Du Bois reflected on all these questions. He took education seriously for at least two (related) reasons: first because it can be a means to social progress (more specifically, to overcoming racism), and second because it can prepare human beings for a life of flourishing.

As with the other thinkers I consider here, social critique that involves diagnosing the failures of the current arrangements is closely tied to thinking about education. The reigning educational (and wider social) arrangements are to be condemned, because under them African Americans are confined by racial injustice. A conception of human flourishing (a life that is "more than meat") and a vision of social justice animate Du Bois's plea for reforming education. His writings enhance our sympathy and moral imagination. They offer a vision of social justice, facilitated by education: "What a world this will be when human possibilities are freed, when we discover each other, when the stranger is no longer the potential criminal and the certain inferior!"[29] As Dewey saw it, taking philosophy of education seriously involves engaging in a wider democratic dialogue that contributes to a larger inquiry into how life is "hemmed in" by the existing arrangements. Du Bois made an essential contribution to this conversation.

§4.6. WHY SHOULD WE CARE?

Although the thinkers considered here often disagreed in their specific ethical, political, and aesthetic doctrines, they nevertheless agreed on making education central to their inquiries into these subjects. In doing so they took education seriously as central to philosophy. This brief overview of the affinities between Plato, Rousseau, Du Bois, and Dewey shows us how addressing questions in prima facie distinct areas of philosophy—exploring racial injustice, the nature of democracy, the value of the arts—can be enriched by focusing on education. Together with these interlocutors, Dewey shows us not only what it would mean to take philosophy of education seriously but also why we need a philosophical stance to educational issues. I have tried to suggest several (related) reasons.

First, we should care about this project if we care about human flourishing, individual and communal, and about finding ways to harmonize the two. For Dewey, as for his interlocutors in the tradition I have been outlining, education was central as "the systematic means by which the good life was to be arrived at and maintained" (1929–30, LW 5:291) on both the individual and the communal levels.[30]

Second, we should care about philosophy of education because it can enrich the way we do philosophy. It can be a means to focus our inquiries once again on central human concerns, and even to connect prima facie distinct areas of philosophy (such as aesthetics and political theory). By taking education seriously, we can make our theorizing relevant to life:

> In fact, education offers a vantage ground from which to penetrate to the human, as distinct from the technical, significance of philosophic discussions. The student of philosophy "in itself" is always in danger of taking it as so much nimble or severe intellectual exercise—as something said by philosophers and concerning them alone. But when philosophic issues are approached from the side of the kind of mental disposition to which they correspond, or the differences in educational practice they make when acted upon, the life-situations which they formulate can never be far from view (1916, MW 9:338).

Like some of his other interlocutors, Dewey imbued his educational theory with a remarkable sensitivity to "all that hems in and distorts human life" (1929–30, LW 5:297–98). Behind Dewey's plea for educational reform was his ardent faith in the possibility of gradually pushing back life's boundaries. We should take philosophy of education seriously if, like Dewey, we care about liberating human capacities:

> When shall we realize that in every school-building in the land a struggle is also being waged against all that hems in and distorts human life? The struggle is not with arms and violence; its consequences cannot be recorded in statistics of the physically killed and wounded, nor set forth in terms of territorial changes. But in its slow and imperceptible processes, the real battles for

human freedom and for the pushing back of the boundaries that restrict human life are ultimately won. We need to pledge ourselves to engage anew and with renewed faith in the greatest of all battles in the cause of human liberation, to the end that all human beings may lead the life that is alone worthy of being entitled wholly human. (1929–30, LW 5:297–98)

Dewey's underappreciated theory of education is still important in our times not just because of its philosophical depth but also because of the continued relevance of the moral vision informing it. The drudgery, confinement, and estrangement that Dewey worried about are still largely with us. His imaginative vision of a world in which such confinement would be gradually overcome still resonates with our "better hopes" (1916, MW 9:85). This brings me to my final point: the importance of the moral imagination to the enterprise.

The thinkers who contributed to the age-old conversation on education "in its largest sense" each appealed to our moral imagination. Think of Plato's defense of the life of inquiry as exemplified by Socrates, captured so unforgettably in the *Apology*. Or Rousseau's dream of living in accordance with nature. Or Du Bois's vision of a world in which "we discover each other" and "the stranger is no longer the potential criminal and the certain inferior."[31] Think of Dewey's hope that one day all of us may lead "a life worth living." All these are voices in a dialogue spanning millennia that have extended our imagination of human possibilities.

The conversation must continue.

NOTES

INTRODUCTION

Throughout this book, when citing John Dewey, I use in-text citations with abbreviations referring to the standard edition of his *Collected Works* (divided into *Early Works*, *Middle Works*, and *Later Works*) published by the University of Southern Illinois Press. These abbreviations include the original publication date of the Dewey text in question, followed by the series and volume number from the standard edition of Dewey's *Collected Works*, followed by the relevant page number(s). For instance, (1920, MW 12:193) refers to page 193 of volume 12 of the *Middle Works*, which contains a piece Dewey originally published in 1920.

1. Plato, *Republic* (Indianapolis: Hackett, 1992), 60–93. Note that although Dewey engaged primarily with the *Republic* among Plato's works, it isn't the only locus of Plato's philosophy of education. For an analysis of the importance of education in Plato's *Laws*, see Randall Curren, "Justice, Instruction, and the Good: The Case for Public Education in Aristotle and Plato's Laws, Part I: Groundwork for an Interpretation of Politics VIII.1," *Studies in Philosophy and Education* 11, no. 4 (1993): 293–311. And then there is Jean-Jacques Rousseau: "See the difference there is already between your pupil's knowledge and mine's ignorance! They know maps, and *he makes them*." *Emile* (New York: Basic Books, 1979), 171, my emphasis.

2. On Plato's ideal curriculum for the rulers as presented in the *Republic*, see Myles F. Burnyeat, "Plato on Why Mathematics Is Good for the Soul," *Proceedings of the British Academy* 103 (2000): 1–81.

3. Rousseau, *Emile*, 43.

4. Some contemporary philosophers have made significant contributions to the field. See, for example, Elizabeth Anderson, "Fair Opportunity in Education: A Democratic Equality Perspective," *Ethics* 117, no. 4 (2007): 595–622; David Bakhurst, *The Formation of Reason* (New York: Wiley-Blackwell, 2011); Harry Brighouse, *On Education* (New York: Routledge, 2006); Randall Curren, "Pragmatist Philosophy of Education," in *The Oxford Handbook of Philosophy of Education*, ed. Harvey Siegel (New York: Oxford University Press, 2009), 489–507; Randall Curren and Charles Dorn, *Patriotic Education in a Global Age* (Chicago: University of Chicago Press, 2018); Catherine Z. Elgin, "Education and the Advancement of Understanding," in *Philosophy of Education*, ed. Randall Curren (Malden, MA: Blackwell, 2007), 417–22; Amy Gutmann, *Democratic Education* (Princeton, NJ: Princeton University Press, 1999); Axel Honneth, "Education and the Democratic Public Sphere: A Neglected Chapter of Political Philosophy," in *Recognition and Freedom: Axel Honneth's Political Thought*, ed. J. Jakobsen and O. Lysaker (Leiden: Brill, 2015), 17–32; Philip S. Kitcher, "Education, Democracy and Capitalism," in *Preludes to Pragmatism: Toward a Reconstruction of Philosophy* (New York: Oxford University Press, 2012), 344–62; Philip S. Kitcher, *The Main Enterprise of the World: Rethinking Education* (Oxford: Oxford University Press, 2021); Anthony Kronman, *Education's End: Why Our Colleges and Universities Have Given up on the Meaning of Life* (New Haven, CT: Yale University Press, 2007); Meira Levinson, *The Demands of Liberal Education* (New York: Oxford University Press, 1999); Meira Levinson, *No Citizen Left Behind* (Cambridge, MA: Harvard University Press, 2012); Michele M. Moody-Adams, "Philosophy and the Art of Human Flourishing," in *Philosophy and Flourishing*, ed. James Stuhr and Joseph Pawelski (New York: Oxford University Press, 2020), 280–300; Martha Nussbaum, *Not for Profit: Why Democracy Needs the Humanities* (Princeton, NJ: Princeton University Press, 2010); Richard S. Peters, "Education as Initiation," in *Philosophy of Education: An Anthology*, ed. Randall Curren (Malden, MA: Blackwell, 2007), 1–4; Harvey Siegel,

"Introduction: Philosophy of Education and Philosophy," in *The Oxford Handbook of Philosophy of Education*, ed. Harvey Siegel (New York: Oxford University Press, 2009), 3–10. Still, philosophy of education remains outside what is seen as the "core" of the discipline.

I. PHILOSOPHY AND EDUCATION

1. My understanding of the variety of characterizations Dewey gave of his philosophy is informed by Philip Kitcher's work on this issue. See Philip S. Kitcher, "Dewey's Conception of Philosophy," in *The Oxford Handbook of Dewey*, ed. Steven Fesmire (Oxford University Press, 2017), 3–22. For example, in *Experience and Nature*, Dewey writes that philosophy is "a critique of prejudices" (1925, LW 1:40) and "a criticism of criticisms" (LW 1, 298–99). In *Reconstruction in Philosophy* he suggests that philosophy has a double task: a "negative" task of criticism, as well as the more "positive" task of imagining new possibilities (1920, MW 12:155). In *The Quest for Certainty*, he says philosophy is "a liaison officer between the conclusions of science and the modes of social and personal action through which attainable possibilities are projected and striven for" (1929, LW 4:248).

2. Dewey's works engage with organized educational practice on all levels, from elementary (e.g., "The Place of Manual Training in the Elementary Course of Study," 1901, MW 1:230–37) to university education (e.g. "A College Course: What Should I Expect from It?," 1890, EW 3:51–55), to lifelong education (this theme is developed in "The School as Social Centre," 1902, MW 2:80–93, among other writings).

3. See, for example, Dewey's rejection of "Platonic Ideas" with their "finished, complete, stable, wholly unprecarious reality" (1925, LW 1:54). Dewey argued against "that striking division into a superior true realm of being and lower illusory, insignificant or phenomenal realm" that characterizes Plato's metaphysics, on his reading (1925, LW 1:55).

We see Dewey arguing against Platonic philosopher-kings in an early essay titled "The Ethics of Democracy" (1888, EW 1:227–49). The argument is continued in *Democracy and Education* (1916, MW 9). In many ways, *The Public and Its Problems* (1927, LW 2:235–372) continues pursuing this theme, targeted at Walter Lippmann, Plato's self-styled modern disciple.

4. Plato, *Republic*, 184–85.

5. "As the children are born, they'll be taken over by the officials appointed for the purpose" (Plato, *Republic*, 134). The city would take "every precaution to ensure that no mother knows her own child" (Plato, *Republic*, 135). See the extensive discussion of poetry and the arts in Books III and X.

6. This reading seems to me consistent with Burnyeat, from whose study I learned a lot. See Myles F. Burnyeat, "Culture and Society in Plato's Republic," The Tanner Lectures on Human Values, delivered at Harvard University, December 10–12, 1997, https://tannerlectures.org/lectures/culture-and-society-in-platos-republic/.

   Of course, there are many ways to read the *Republic*. Throughout the ages, readers with widely different philosophical agendas have found resources in Plato to advance their own visions. What I am concerned with here isn't outlining "the definitive reading," but showing what Plato might look like if seen primarily as an educational theorist. Dewey read Plato this way. So did Rousseau. In *Emile*, Rousseau says that the *Republic* "is not at all a political work, as think those who judge books only by their titles" (Rousseau, *Emile*, 40). Certainly, one might object that these readings were selective—they served specific philosophical agendas. This, too, is part of the story I want to tell. Dewey and Rousseau both construed Plato as a philosopher of education. Whether or not they captured the whole of Plato's thought, their conversations with him are part of the tradition of taking education seriously.

7. There are exceptions. Some contemporary philosophers take education seriously and have made significant contributions to it. See, for example, Elizabeth Anderson, "Fair Opportunity in Education: A Democratic Equality Perspective," *Ethics* 117, no. 4 (2007): 595–622; David Bakhurst, *The Formation of Reason* (New York: Wiley-Blackwell, 2011); Harry Brighouse, *On Education* (New York: Routledge, 2006); Randall Curren, "Pragmatist Philosophy of Education," in *The Oxford Handbook of Philosophy of Education*, ed. Harvey Siegel (New York: Oxford University Press, 2009), 489–507; Randall Curren and Roger Dorn, *Patriotic Education in a Global Age* (Chicago: University of Chicago Press, 2018); Catherine Z. Elgin, "Education and the

Advancement of Understanding," in *Philosophy of Education*, ed. Randall Curren (Malden, MA: Blackwell, 2009), 417–22; Amy Gutmann, *Democratic Education* (Princeton, NJ: Princeton University Press, 1999); Axel Honneth, "Education and the Democratic Public Sphere: A Neglected Chapter of Political Philosophy," In *Recognition and Freedom: Axel Honneth's Political Thought*, ed. J. Jakobsen and O. Lysaker (Leiden: Brill, 2015), 17–32; Philip S. Kitcher, *Preludes to Pragmatism: Toward a Reconstruction of Philosophy* (New York: Oxford University Press, 2012), 58–74, and *The Main Enterprise of the World: Rethinking Education* (New York: Oxford University Press, 2021); Anthony Kronman, *Education's End: Why Our Colleges and Universities Have Given up on the Meaning of Life* (New Haven, CT: Yale University Press, 2007); Meira Levinson, *The Demands of Liberal Education* (New York: Oxford University Press, 1999), and *No Citizen Left Behind* (Cambridge, MA: Harvard University Press, 2012); Michele Moody-Adams, "Philosophy and the Art of Human Flourishing," in *Philosophy and Flourishing*, ed. James Stuhr and Joseph Pawelski (New York: Oxford University Press, 2020), 214–30; Martha Nussbaum, *Not for Profit: Why Democracy Needs the Humanities* (Princeton, NJ: Princeton University Press, 2010); Richard S. Peters, "Education as Initiation," in *Philosophy of Education: An Anthology*, ed. Randall Curren (Malden, MA: Blackwell, 2007), 1–4; and Harvey Siegel, "Introduction: Philosophy of Education and Philosophy," in *The Oxford Handbook of Philosophy of Education*, ed. Harvey Siegel (New York: Oxford University Press, 2009), 3–10.

8. For Dewey's views on Darwin, see "The Influence of Darwinism on Philosophy" (1909, MW 4:3–14). Dewey also claimed that he owed a great deal to William James: "As far as I can discover one specifiable philosophic factor which entered into my thinking so as to give it a new direction and quality, it is this one." James's *Principles of Psychology* had a particularly big influence. The book was important to Dewey in part, he continued, because of its "biological conception of the *psyche*. . . . It worked its way more and more into all my ideas and acted as a ferment to transform old beliefs" (1930, LW 5:157).

9. Plato may not have been a "Simple Platonist." Focusing on the relationship between Plato's educational and political theory in the *Laws*,

Randall Curren argues for a reaching on which Plato had "a kind of consent theory." Curren, "Justice, Instruction, and the Good: The Case for Public Education in Aristotle and Plato's Laws, Part III—Why Education Should Be Public and the Same for All," *Studies in Philosophy and Education* 13, no. 1 (1994): 1–31, at 21. Analyzing Plato's proposals regarding preludes to the laws, Curren writes: "These preludes must precede not only the laws as a whole, but each of them individually, Plato insists (723B), and the inference we must draw is that his suggestion is that it is largely through this means, and the education of the capacities of reason already mentioned, that the legislator will endeavor to obtain the consent of the citizens to his or her rule, that being a mode of rule in which the laws are sovereign and worthy of consent, since they aim at the common good. They are laws for which sufficient reasons exist, and the aim of the preludes is to state those reasons in a rhetorically effective way" (21). Another way to resist the "Simple Platonist" picture is to focus on the "negative," ironic Socrates, emphasizing his disavowal of knowledge and the self-undermining nature of the Platonic dialogues that end in aporia. Interestingly, Dewey was no stranger to reading Plato this way: at one point, he said that he actually preferred "the dramatic, restless, cooperatively inquiring Plato of the *Dialogues*" (1930, LW 5:155) to the systematic philosopher that scholars often see in him. But when it came to formulating his own views, Dewey often took the proposals found in the *Republic* at face value, as he did in *Democracy and Education* (1916, MW 9:97). For a reading that seems to be close to the "Simple Platonist" view, see Myles F. Burnyeat, "Plato on Why Mathematics Is Good for the Soul," *Proceedings of the British Academy* 103 (2000): 1–81. For a view that prioritizes the picture of Socrates as an ironist, see Alexander Nehamas, *The Art of Living: Socratic Reflections from Plato to Foucault* (Berkeley: University of California Press, 1998).

10. My understanding of Dewey on this point is indebted to conversations with Philip Kitcher. See, for example, Philip S. Kitcher, "Social Progress," *Social Philosophy and Policy* 34, no. 2 (2017): 46–65.

11. I borrow this phrase from Walter Lippmann's critique of the hopes democratic theorists put in education: "the usual appeal to education as the remedy for the incompetence of democracy is . . . barren. It is,

in effect, a proposal that school teachers shall *by some magic of their own* fit men to govern after the makers of laws and the preachers of civic ideals have had a free hand in writing the specifications. . . . The usual appeal to education can bring only disappointment." Lippmann, *The Phantom Public* (New Brunswick, NJ: Transaction Publishers, 1993), 16–17, my emphasis.

12. My reading of Plato on this point is indebted to Burnyeat, "Culture and Society in Plato's Republic."

13. W. E. B. Du Bois, *The Souls of Black Folk*, ed. David W. Blight and Robert Gooding-Williams (New York: Bedford/St. Martin's, 1997), 36.

14. Du Bois, *The Souls of Black Folk*, 41.

15. Dewey's view on this aligns (at least in broad outlines) with some recent historical scholarship. On philosophy as a way of life in the ancient tradition, see, for instance, John M. Cooper, *Six Ways of Life in Ancient Philosophy from Socrates to Plotinus* (Princeton, NJ: Princeton University Press, 2012).

16. For an exploration of philosophy as a personal way of life, see Nehamas, *The Art of Living*. Nehamas focuses on how various philosophers seek to cultivate their individual uniqueness through the use of Socratic irony. By contrast, Dewey's main concern was not with philosophy as a private, individual pursuit, but with how it influences broader practices, institutions and discourses that shape us.

17. Georg Wilhelm Friedrich Hegel, *Elements of the Philosophy of Right*, ed. Allen W. Wood, trans. H. B. Nisbet (Cambridge: Cambridge University Press, 1991), 22.

18. I see my reconstruction of the way in which Dewey's conception of philosophy as theory of education might fit with his other characterizations of philosophy as complementary to Philip S. Kitcher's argument that the different characterizations of philosophy are connected, but that they might emphasize different aspects of Dewey's understanding of philosophy. See Kitcher, "Dewey's Conception of Philosophy."

19. Plato, *Republic*, trans. G. M. A. Grube and C. D. C. Reeve (Indianapolis: Hackett, 1992), 134–35.

20. This is done in Philip S. Kitcher's work. See, for example, *Moral Progress* (New York: Oxford University Press, 2021).

21. Quoted in Burnyeat, "Plato on Why Mathematics Is Good for the Soul," 80 (my emphasis). Burnyeat uses this passage to argue that Plato was a deeply paradoxical philosopher who formulated an unusual conception of the good that was entirely at odds with common opinion.

22. As with any great philosopher, there are many ways to read Hegel. Here I am concerned only with Dewey's own reading. *Reconstruction in Philosophy* explicitly criticizes Hegel for employing philosophy to justify the status quo (1920, MW 12:90). On reconciliation, see Hegel, *Elements of the Philosophy of Right*, 22. Friedrich Nietzsche criticizes Hegelian philosophical culture eloquently in "On the Uses and Disadvantages of History for Life." Nietzsche, *Untimely Meditations*, ed. Daniel Breazeale, trans. R. J. Hollingdale (New York: Cambridge University Press, 1997), 57–124.

23. Plutarch reports that the Stoic Chrysippus "extravagantly praises Homer" for saying this. See Plutarch, *On Stoic Self-Contradictions*, quoted in A. A. Long and D. N. Sedley, *The Hellenistic Philosophers* (Cambridge: Cambridge University Press, 2015), 339.

24. When he formulated this view, Dewey may well have been thinking of the famous passage in the *Philosophy of Right* where Hegel writes: "A further word on the subject of *issuing instructions* on how the world ought to be: philosophy, at any rate, always comes too late to perform this function. . . . It appears only at a time when actuality has gone through its formative process and attained its complete state. . . . When philosophy paints its grey in grey, a shape of life has grown old, and it cannot be rejuvenated, but only understood, by the grey in grey of philosophy; the owl of Minerva begins its flight only with the onset of dusk." Hegel, *Elements of the Philosophy of Right*, 23.

25. Alan Ryan, *John Dewey and the High Tide of American Liberalism* (New York: W. W. Norton, 1995), 34.

26. My reading of Dewey on this point seems to resonate with Cheryl Misak's understanding of important pragmatist themes in American thought, particularly as exemplified in the writings of Peirce and Royce. See Misak, *The American Pragmatists* (New York: Oxford University Press, 2013). I thank her for bringing this to my attention.

27. For a related critique, see also Ryan, *John Dewey and the High Tide of American Liberalism*.

2. DEMOCRACY AND EDUCATION

I would like to thank Robert Gooding-Williams, Axel Honneth, Michele M. Moody-Adams, and Philip Kitcher for inspiring discussions and helpful suggestions about the issues I consider here.

1. Plato, *Republic*, 233, 236.
2. In appreciating the importance of Dewey's debate with Lippmann, I have benefited from conversations with Michele M. Moody-Adams. On the Dewey-Lippmann debate, see also James Bohman, "Participation Through Publics: Did Dewey Answer Lippmann?," *Contemporary Pragmatism* 7, no. 1 (2010): 49–68; Matthew Festenstein, "Does Dewey Have an 'Epistemic Argument' for Democracy?," *Contemporary Pragmatism* 16, no. 2–3 (2019): 217–41; Melvin L. Rogers, "Dewey and His Vision of Democracy," *Contemporary Pragmatism* 7, no. 1 (2010): 69–91. Existing scholarship on the Dewey-Lippmann debate focuses primarily on issues of epistemic justification and expertise. My study aims to add to this literature by focusing on a different angle: democratic education.

   Inspired by William James, Lippmann's analysis of stereotypes in *Public Opinion* (originally published in 1922) was pioneering for its time. See, for example, Walter Lippmann, *Public Opinion* (New York: Free Press, 1997), 54–55.
3. See, for example, "Democracy Is Radical," where he rejected "any other than liberal democratic means" to achieve radical social ends. Among other things, he wrote: "The idea that those who possess power never surrender it save when forced to do so by superior physical power, applies to *dictatorships that claim to operate in behalf of the oppressed masses while actually operating to wield power against the masses*" (1937, LW 11:298, my emphasis).
4. Already in 1939, Dewey worried about the complacency of his contemporaries: "the depth of the present crisis is due in considerable part to the fact that for a long period we acted as if our democracy were something that perpetuated itself automatically . . . We acted as if democracy were something that took place mainly in Washington and Albany—or some other state capital—under the impetus of what happened when men and women went to the polls once a year or

so—which is a somewhat extreme way of saying that we have had the habit of thinking of democracy as a kind of political mechanism that will work as long as citizens were reasonably faithful in performing political duties" (1939, LW 14:225).

5. Dewey's critique is directed at the mainstream mindset within philosophy departments. The worry is that philosophers working within them often don't take education seriously as a central philosophical issue. Of course, important work on education is being done by philosophers of education working in education departments, teachers thinking about philosophical issues, as well as virtue ethicists and virtue epistemologists (whose concerns overlap with Dewey's). I thank the anonymous reviewer for prompting me to clarify this point.

6. Plato, *Republic*, 170.

7. See chapter 1, note 7.

8. Dewey's conception of democratic schooling went far beyond teaching "civics." He explicitly argues against focusing exclusively on "civics" in "The School as Social Centre" (MW 2:80–94).

9. A number of contributions to scholarship on Deweyan democracy focus on issues of epistemic justification. For example, Matthew Festenstein considers whether Dewey had "an epistemic argument for democracy" and argues that his thought provides "potential resources for the epistemic democrat." Festenstein, "Does Dewey Have an 'Epistemic Argument' for Democracy?," 217–41. Cheryl Misak focuses on the relationship between democracy and inquiry and argues that Dewey contributes to the "epistemic justification of a democratic method of inquiry" that has roots in Peirce and James. Misak, *The American Pragmatists* (New York: Oxford University Press, 2013), 136. Other contributions focus on the "epistemic division of labor" in Deweyan democracy (see Bohman, "Participation Through Publics") and on issues of expertise (Rogers, "Dewey and His Vision of Democracy"). Some debate the relationship between Deweyan democracy and pluralism. See the debate between Rogers and Talisse in Robert B. Talisse, "A Farewell to Deweyan Democracy," *Political Studies* 59 (2011): 509–26; Melvin L. Rogers, "Dewey, Pluralism, and Democracy: A Response to Robert Talisse," *Transactions of the Charles S. Peirce Society* 45, no. 1 (2009): 75–79. My focus here is different. I take myself to be adding to the existing literature by examining specifically the connection between

democracy and *education* in Dewey's thought. Another set of literature discusses Dewey's conception of democratic education; see, for example, Steven Fesmire, *Dewey* (New York: Routledge, 2015), and Jeff Jackson, *Equality Beyond Debate: John Dewey's Pragmatic Idea of Democracy* (New York: Cambridge University Press, 2018).

10. On the centrality of education to political philosophy, see also Honneth, "Education and the Democratic Public Sphere: A Neglected Chapter of Political Philosophy," in *Recognition and Freedom: Axel Honneth's Political Thought*, ed. J. Jakobsen and O. Lysaker (Leiden: Brill, 2015), 17–32. I view my argument here as complementary.

11. Plato, *Republic*, 231–32.

12. Plato, *Republic*, 169.

13. Here, as in chapter 1, I read Plato as a Simple Platonist (taking what Socrates says in the *Republic* at face value), not because I think this is the best reading (it probably isn't) but because it helps clarify Dewey's thought. This is how Dewey would have read him. Even if Plato didn't hold the views considered by Socrates in the *Republic*, those views are thought-provoking and worth introducing into the conversation.

14. Rousseau, *Emile*, 40.

15. Rousseau, *Emile*, 251.

16. For an analysis of the inadequacy of the early organicist metaphors in Dewey's "The Ethics of Democracy," as well as of some of the specific ways in which Dewey in *The Public and Its Problems* moved away from these metaphors in favor of a more naturalistic understanding of social progress and a more pluralistic understanding of community life, see Melvin L. Rogers, "Revisiting *The Public and Its Problems*," in *The Public and Its Problems*, ed. Melvin L. Rogers (Athens, OH: Swallow Press, 2016), 10–15.

17. Dewey actually used the expression "inward grace" to describe "the democratic spirit" in the context of discussing democratic architecture: "Our public buildings may become the outward and visible sign of the inward grace which is the democratic spirit" ("Art as Our Heritage"; 1940, LW 14:257).

18. It is important to note that Dewey resisted the idea of molding human beings into *fixed* "types." That was precisely one of his objections against totalitarian societies: they attempt to create a

"fixed predetermined type" of human being ("Unpublished Writings";
LW 17: 478). He resisted not only the idea that human beings should be
molded into fixed, predetermined types, but also that they naturally fall
into fixed types. He took this to be an important—false—assumption
of "Platonic" political theory (1888, EW 1:243–44; 1916, MW 9:96).

19. Even Alan Ryan, one of Dewey's most perceptive and charitable read-
ers, dismisses his emphasis on growth as "obsessive." See Ryan, *John
Dewey and the High Tide of American Liberalism* (New York: W. W.
Norton, 1995).

20. Rousseau, *Emile*, 286.

21. Of course, much more can still be said about wider social growth. As
chapter 1 points out, Dewey himself never gave us all the details. For
a further account, see Kitcher, "Dewey's Conception of Philosophy."

22. Richard Bernstein worries that Dewey "never indicated in detail" what
economic changes should take place to realize his democratic ideal and
what the specific details of his "inclusive plan" for liberalism are. Bernstein, *The Pragmatic Turn* (London: Polity Press, 2010). It is true that
Dewey was often tantalizingly vague about the specifics of the social
and economic reforms he called for. However, it would be entirely in
keeping with his understanding of inquiry to say that he saw himself
as identifying prejudices that stand in the way of further inquiry—to
be conducted not only by philosophers, but, crucially, by democratic
citizens in consultation with each other. It is democratic dialogue that
should determine what the specific reforms should be, and not any
single philosopher.

23. Jean-Jacques Rousseau, *The Reveries of the Solitary Walker*, trans.
Charles E. Butterworth (Indianapolis: Hackett, 1992), 12, 69, my
emphasis.

24. Jean-Jacques Rousseau, "Discourse on the Origin of Inequality," in
Basic Political Writings, trans. and ed. David A. Cress (Indianapolis:
Hackett, 1987), 33.

25. On these aspects of Rousseau's thought, see Frederick Neuhouser,
*Rousseau's Theodicy of Self-Love: Evil, Rationality, and the Drive for Rec-
ognition* (New York: Oxford University Press, 2008).

26. Rousseau's *Emile* might be read as aiming at this goal, too. However,
the initial step is to strip away all social influence as much as possible—
"keeping the nascent shrub away from the highway" (38). This couldn't

be further from Dewey's position. Unlike Rousseau's program, Dewey's doesn't seek to get to the bedrock of an "original self" at the get-go. He seeks immersion in social life—the sort that would help develop one's individuality.

27. Dewey's appreciation of the importance of recognition (e.g., 1925, LW 1:187–88) can be connected to strands in Hegel's thinking, as well as to contemporary work on recognition. See, for example, Axel Honneth, *The I in We: Studies in the Theory of Recognition* (London: Polity Press, 2012); and Frederick Neuhouser, *Foundations of Hegel's Social Theory: Actualizing Freedom* (Cambridge, MA: Harvard University Press, 2000), and *Rousseau's Theodicy of Self-Love*. However, Dewey wasn't just an uncritical proponent of Hegelianism. He thought that Hegel's view did not allow enough room for individuals to transform social institutions, and he rejected the idea that social progress is in some sense "organic" (1916, MW 9:65). On the relationship between Dewey and Hegel, see also Bernstein, *The Pragmatic Turn*, 91–92; Stephen Rockefeller, *John Dewey: Religious Faith and Democratic Humanism* (New York: Columbia University Press, 1991), 236–37.

28. Rousseau, *The Reveries of the Solitary Walker*, 69.

29. Rousseau, *Emile*, 474. Book V of *Emile* paints Rousseau's vision of the rustic utopia—"the most natural," "patriarchal and rustic life"—in which Emile and Sophie are destined to live.

30. The Romantic conception of a lost original self is eloquently articulated in Rousseau's *Discourse on the Origin of Inequality*: "And how will man be successful in seeing himself *as nature formed him*, through all the changes that the succession of time and things must have produced in his *original constitution*, and in separating what he derives from his own wherewithal from what circumstances and his progress have added to or changed in his *primitive state*? Like the statue of Glaucus, which time, sea and storms had disfigured to such an extent that it looks less like a god than a wild beast, the human soul, *altered in the midst of society* by a thousand constantly recurring causes, by the acquisition of a multitude of bits of knowledge and of errors, by changes that took place in the constitution of bodies, by the constant impact of the passions, has, as it were, changed its appearance to the point of being nearly unrecognizable." Rousseau, "Discourse on the Origin of Inequality," 33, my emphases.

31. Rousseau saw his *Emile* as an attempt to revive a lost "golden age" by painting the charms of what a life in harmony with nature would look like: "The golden age is treated as a chimera, and it will always be one for anyone whose heart and taste have been spoiled. It is not even true that people regret the golden age, since those regrets are always hollow. What, then, would be required to give it a new birth? One single but impossible thing: to love it" (474).

32. Although she doesn't engage much with Dewey, there are interesting resonances between these aspects of Dewey's thought and Rahel Jaeggi's work on articulating a concept of alienation without resorting to the idea of an "essential" self. Jaeggi, *Alienation* (New York: Columbia University Press, 2014).

33. Plato, *Complete Works*, ed. John M. Cooper (Indianapolis: Hackett, 1997), 503.

34. In formulating a view on this, I am indebted to conversations with Philip Kitcher. On this point, see Kitcher, *The Main Enterprise of the World: Rethinking Education* (New York: Oxford University Press, 2021).

35. Alan Ryan charged Dewey with ignoring the value of "ethical individualism" (*John Dewey and the High Tide of American Liberalism*, 148–49). The charge isn't fair. Dewey extolled the value of creative, critical engagement with society on the part of individuals. Still, we can formulate a more moderate version of Ryan's worry. The danger is that Dewey's emphasis on the value of social immersion for cultivating individuality *leaves him with fewer resources* to defend the importance of "ethical individualism"—the choice to suffer "estrangement" from one's community "when sufficient intellectual or moral reasons demand it" (148–49). One might defend one's choice for "ethical individualism" by appealing to the voice of an "original" self. Rousseau's *Reveries* adopts this strategy. But it isn't available to Dewey. He tried to preserve the idea that individuality is to be valued by suggesting that organisms have some "irreducible uniqueness" (1925, LW 1:187). Expressing it is central to personal flourishing and might even aid communal growth as variations introduced by individuals challenge prevailing habits. But the notion is still fuzzy. He exactly do the "native tendencies" of the

individual develop under the influences of social life? How does the need for social connectedness interact with the need for autonomy in the development of individuality? Dewey gives no clear answers.

36. For a reconstruction of Rousseau's solution to this problem, see Neuhouser, *Rousseau's Theodicy of Self-Love*.

37. Plato, *Republic*, 148.

38. This is why I focus more on the *methodology* for Deweyan democratic growth—i.e. the features of democratic dialogue required to achieve it—than on its specific outcomes. The fundamental difference between Plato and Dewey is that Plato thought philosophers could formulate a conception of the "good" apart from the input of democratic citizens; Dewey's vision was exactly the opposite. The purpose of Deweyan democratic education was to empower citizens to engage in dialogue that would allow *them* to formulate directions for democratic growth in prejudice-overcoming dialogue and sympathetic mutual engagement. I thank the anonymous reviewer for comments that prompted me to clarify this point.

39. Plato, *Republic*, 233.

40. On the importance of critical thinking to democratic education, see Randall Curren and Charles Dorn, *Patriotic Education in a Global Age* (Chicago: University of Chicago Press, 2018).

41. This central facet of Dewey's conception of democracy—and the (related) idea that democracy is educative—is my focus here. It is worth noting that in different contexts Dewey emphasized somewhat different (albeit related) facets of democracy. Some writings focus on democracy as a way of life rather than a set of institutions (1888, EW 1:240; 1902, MW 2:82–83; 1939, LW 14:226). Others illuminate the value of genuine democratic dialogue (1927, LW 2:350; 1950, LW 17:86). Still others probe the relationship between democracy and inquiry, including social science and communal inquiry (1927, LW 2:339; 1939, LW 14:229). Some pieces explore the aesthetic aspects of vitally shared social life (1920, MW 12:200), while others focus on the experimental (1927, LW 2:256–57) and creative (1939, LW 14:225) aspects of democracy. Industrial democracy is sometimes in the foreground (1941, LW 14:263). The centrality of cooperation to democracy is another important subject (1950, LW 17:87). As is, of course, my topic here: democracy's

educative effects (1916, MW 9:93; 1920, MW 12:199–200; 1927, LW 2:364; 1950, LW17:86).

42. On these creative aspects of democracy, see also Richard Bernstein, "Creative Democracy—The Task Still Before Us," *American Journal of Theology and Philosophy* 21, no. 3 (2000): 226. For other commentaries on Dewey's conception of democracy, see also Bernstein, *The Pragmatic Turn*; Gregory F. Pappas, *John Dewey's Ethics: Democracy as Experience* (Bloomington: Indiana University Press, 2008); Stephen Rockefeller, *John Dewey: Religious Faith and Democratic Humanism* (New York: Columbia University Press, 1991); Rogers, "Revisiting *The Public and Its Problems*"; Ryan, *John Dewey and the High Tide of American Liberalism*; Charlene H. Seigfried, "Socializing Democracy: Jane Addams and John Dewey," *Philosophy of the Social Sciences* 29, no. 2 (1999): 207–30; and Robert Westbrook, *John Dewey and American Democracy* (Ithaca, NY: Cornell University Press, 1991).

43. On the importance of communicative skills to democratic education, see also Elizabeth Anderson, "Fair Opportunity in Education: A Democratic Equality Perspective," *Ethics* 117, no. 4 (2007): 595–622.

44. The arts are important for exercising and developing such capacities (1934, LW 10). On the importance of the arts for the development of human capacities and for democracy, see also Michele M. Moody-Adams, "Civic Art of Remembrance and the Democratic Imagination," 56th Annual Bishop Hurst Lecture, American University, 2015; Michele M. Moody-Adams, "Philosophy and the Art of Human Flourishing," in *Philosophy and Flourishing*, ed. James Stuhr and Joseph Pawelski (New York: Oxford University Press, 2020), 214–30; and Martha Nussbaum, *Not for Profit: Why Democracy Needs the Humanities* (Princeton, NJ: Princeton University Press, 2010).

45. Other scholars have also recognized the importance of communication and of humility to Deweyan democracy. On communication, see Matthew Festenstein, "The Ties of Communication: Dewey on Ideal and Political Democracy," *History of Political Thought* 18, no. 1 (1997): 104–24. On humility and openness to different points of view, see Rogers, "Dewey, Pluralism, and Democracy," 78. My analysis aims to add to their important contributions by considering these issues in the context of reconstructing Dewey's account of democratic education.

46. On the emancipatory aspects of Dewey's conception of democracy, see, for example, Charlene H. Seigfried, "Socializing Democracy: Jane Addams and John Dewey," *Philosophy of the Social Sciences* 29, no. 2 (1999): 207–30. Seigfried argues that Dewey was deeply influenced by Jane Addams (in particular, by her work at the Hull House Settlement) in formulating his conception of democracy.

47. Lippmann, *Public Opinion*, 79.

48. For an account of the influence of the Hull House settlement and Jane Addams on Dewey's conception of democracy, see Seigfried, "Socializing Democracy: Jane Addams and John Dewey," 207–30.

49. See, for example (among others), Anderson, "Fair Opportunity in Education," 595–622; Curren and Dorn, *Patriotic Education in a Global Age*; Gutmann, *Democratic Education*; Honneth, "Education and the Democratic Public Sphere," 17–32; Kitcher, "Education, Democracy and Capitalism," 58–74; Kitcher, *The Main Enterprise of the World: Rethinking Education*; Levinson, *The Demands of Liberal Education*; Levinson, *No Citizen Left Behind*; Nussbaum, *Not for Profit*.

50. On the historical context in which Dewey developed his ideas on vocational education, see Westbrook, *John Dewey and American Democracy*, 173–74. As Westbrook notes, Dewey's understanding of what vocational education should look like was radically different from that of some of his contemporaries. In particular, Dewey resisted the idea that vocational education should be narrowly focused on preparing human beings for predetermined and sometimes uncongenial and unfulfilling jobs. On Dewey's critique of industrial training, see also Steven Fesmire, "Democracy and the Industrial Imagination in American Education," *Education and Culture* 32, no. 1 (2016): 53–61.

51. Although these concerns in Dewey's writings resonate with Marx's discussion of alienation, it doesn't seem likely that Dewey developed them by reading Marx (since Marx's *Economic and Philosophic Manuscripts of 1844* was released only in 1932). See Karl Marx, *Economic and Philosophic Manuscripts of 1844* (Buffalo, NY: Prometheus Books, 1988). I am indebted to Philip Kitcher in appreciating this point.

52. Du Bois, *The Souls of Black Folk*, 36.

53. On the affinities between Du Bois's and Dewey's commitments to the development of rich personalities, see also Paul C. Taylor, "Beauty to

Set the World Right," in *Black Is Beautiful: A Philosophy of Black Aesthetics* (New York: Wiley, 2016), 92.

54. As mentioned earlier, Alan Ryan provides one example: the need to suffer estrangement from others "for intellectual or moral reasons." Ryan, *John Dewey and the High Tide of American Liberalism*, 148–49.

55. In interpreting Dewey this way, I am indebted to Kitcher. See Kitcher, "Dewey's Conception of Philosophy"; Kitcher, "Social Progress."

56. Plato, *Republic*, 231–32.

57. Plato, *Republic*, 170.

58. Walt Whitman, *Democratic Vistas: The Original Edition in Facsimile*, ed. Ed Folsom (Iowa City: University of Iowa Press, 2010), 33, my emphasis. This bears a striking resemblance to Dewey's call to make democracy a "wider reality:" "The idea of democracy is a wider and fuller idea than can be exemplified in the state even at its best. To be realized it must affect *all modes of human association*, the family, the school, industry, religion" (1927, LW 2:325, my emphasis). On the connection between Whitman and Dewey, see also Richard Rorty, "American National Pride: Whitman and Dewey," in *Achieving Our Country* (Cambridge, MA: Harvard University Press, 1998).

59. See Lippmann, *The Phantom Public* and *Public Opinion*.

3. ART AND EDUCATION

1. Roger Fry, *Vision and Design* (Oxford: Oxford University Press, 1981), 33.

2. Clive Bell, *Art* (New York: Capricorn Books, [1914] 1958), 31, 266. For an account of the abiding influence that Roger Fry and Clive Bell had on modern aesthetics, see Alexander Nehamas, *Only a Promise of Happiness: The Place of Beauty in a World of Art* (Princeton, NJ: Princeton University Press, 2007).

3. Bell, *Art*, 267, 25, 31–32.

4. For a philosophical account of the value of art that follows Dewey in seeking to restore the continuity between art and everyday experience, see also Michele Moody-Adams, "Philosophy and the Art of Human Flourishing," in *Philosophy and Flourishing*, ed. James Stuhr and Joseph Pawelski (New York: Oxford University Press, 2020), 214–30. I have

learned much from conversations with Michele M. Moody-Adams and from her work on these issues.

5. For instance, see the analysis of how modern industrial capitalist societies shortchange artists: "Because of changes in industrial conditions the artist has been pushed to one side from the main streams of active interest. Industry has been mechanized and he cannot work mechanically for mass production" (1934; LW 10: 15).

6. Dewey writes: "There must then be historic reasons for the rise of the compartmental conception of fine art. Our present museums and galleries to which works of fine art are removed and stored illustrate some of the causes that have operated to segregate art instead of finding it an attendant of temple, forum, and other forms of associated life" (1934, LW 10:14). Later he continues: "theories which isolate art and its appreciation by placing them in a realm of their own . . . are not inherent in the subject-matter but arise because of specifiable extraneous conditions" (1934, LW 10:16).

7. Fry, *Vision and Design*, 33.

8. Bell, *Art*, 266–67, 242–43. The last passage is worth quoting in full: "to take art seriously is to be unable to take seriously the conventions and principles by which societies exist. It may be said with some justice that Post-Impressionism is peculiarly anarchical because it insists so emphatically on fundamentals and challenges so violently the conventional tradition of art and, by implication, I suppose, the conventional view of life. *By setting art so high, it sets industrial civilisation very low.* Here, then, it may shake hands with the broader and vaguer spirit of the age; the effort to produce serious art may bear witness to a stir in the underworld, to a weariness of smug materialism and a more passionate and spiritual conception of life" (my emphasis).

9. We should also keep in mind that Dewey didn't argue that the experience that a work of fine art might give us is *identical* in all respects to the aesthetic phases of experience in other settings (such as that of "the grace of the ball-player"), but only that there's some kind of *continuity* between the two (more on this below). In his response to Patrick Romanell, a critic who objected that Dewey in *Art as Experience* has two different notions of the aesthetic (one for fine art and one for ordinary experience), Dewey replied "I certainly do . . . speak of two

forms or sorts of aesthetic experience," but they are continuous—one grows out of the other. Dewey distinguished between the "primary phase" of aesthetic experience and its "artistic development" and said that "my theory holds also that the arts and their aesthetic experience are intentionally cultivated developments of this primary aesthetic phase" (1949, LW 16:395). He even said that "this matter of development of the artistic way or form out of a primary aesthetic phase is the 'heart, soul, and mind' (intention) of the entire book" (1949, LW 16:395–96).

10. Perhaps this point connects Dewey's concerns with Nehamas's. See *Only a Promise of Happiness.* Dewey resisted the idea that the province of art must be so narrowly circumscribed as to exclude what we might find moving and/or beautiful in "ordinary" circumstances, what speaks to us as human beings (not just as "artists").

11. Another passage further clarifies Dewey's view: "Before an artist can develop his reconstruction of the scene before him in terms of the relations of colors and lines characteristic of his picture, he observes the scene with meanings and values brought to his perception by prior experiences. *These are indeed remade, transformed, as his new esthetic vision takes shape.* But they cannot *vanish* and yet the artist continue to see an object" (1934, LW 10:95, my emphases).

12. Fry, *Vision and Design*, 33.

13. Bell, *Art*, 25, my emphasis.

14. Dewey was particularly interested in exploring how the past may enrich our experience of the present: "Every living experience owes its richness to what Santayana well calls 'hushed reverberations'" (1934, LW 10:23). He quoted from George Eliot to underscore the effect that past experience might have on the present: "Our delight in the sunshine on the deep-bladed grass to-day might be no more than the faint perception of wearied souls, were it not for the sunshine and grass of far-off years, which still live in us and transform our perception into love" (1934, LW 10:23–24n1). As we shall see, the effect of the past on present experience isn't always positive—sometimes it may result in the creation of routine, confining habits. In appreciating the way that past experience shapes the present, Dewey may have been inspired by James's *Principles of Psychology*.

15. William James, *Principles of Psychology* (Cambridge, MA: Harvard University Press, 1983), 420.

16. James, *Principles of Psychology*, 420.

17. For a contemporary account that resonates with Dewey's view on how the arts can expand our appreciation of the world around us, see Moody-Adams, "Philosophy and the Art of Human Flourishing."

18. See Richard Kendall in Claude Monet, *Monet by Himself*, ed. Richard Kendall (New York: Bulfinch Press/Little, Brown and Company, 1989), 170.

19. Claude Monet, quoted in Virginia Spate, *Claude Monet: The Color of Time* (London: Thames and Hudson, 1992), 226.

20. Monet, *Monet by Himself*, 179.

21. Spate, *Claude Monet*, 226.

22. Monet, quoted in Spate, *Claude Monet*, 226.

23. Monet's popularity in our day makes it hard to believe that not everyone was ready to accept his radical departure from existing schemes and techniques at the time when he first exhibited the series. Many were "hostile to the application of this mode of painting to a religious monument." As Pissarro notes in his review (Spate, *Claude Monet*, 230), even admirers of Monet opposed the series.

24. "At Rouen Monet severed the facade from the building, the building from its surroundings, and the cathedral *from the meanings history had given it.*" Spate, *Claude Monet*, 226, my emphasis.

25. Interestingly, Spate contrasts Monet's vision with that of mere "identification": "Monet's desire to paint without 'knowing what he saw' was impossible fully to realize; nevertheless, while painting, he had been able to transcend the practical faculty of identification, and to scrutinize his field of vision in terms of 'sensations of colour which give light.' This mode of seeing resulted in images composed of constantly shifting webs of colour whose temporary stabilization into recognizable forms is dependent only on the spectator's desire for the known," Spate, *Claude Monet*, 310.

26. Pissarro quoted in Spate, *Claude Monet*, 230.

27. Pissarro quoted in Spate, *Claude Monet*, 230.

28. For instance, Monet's vision ignores, to a large extent, much of the historical and religious symbolism of the cathedral to focus on the

evanescent effects of light. On this point, see Spate, *Claude Monet*, 226. Ignoring these features isn't something that the audience has to do when engaging with Monet, since they are already largely absent from the paintings.

29. Rainer Maria Rilke, *The Poetry of Rilke*, trans. Edward Snow (Berkeley, CA: North Point Press, 2009), 308–9.

30. For a defense of "moderate egalitarianism" in defining a classic work of art, see Philip S. Kitcher, *The Main Enterprise of the World: Rethinking Education* (New York: Oxford University Press, 2021). Kitcher argues that education should guide the young in finding works of art that speak most to them.

31. *Experience and Nature* echoes the idea: "a genuinely esthetic object is not exclusively consummatory but is causally productive as well. A consummatory object that is not also instrumental turns in time to the dust and ashes of boredom. The 'eternal' quality of great art is its renewed instrumentality for further consummatory experiences" (1925, LW 1:274).

32. Marcel Proust, *Days of Reading*, trans. James Sturrock (New York: Penguin Books, 2008), 71–72.

33. Bell, *Art*, 37, 278.

34. Fry, *Vision and Design*, 33.

35. In addition to engaging with his contemporaries, Dewey also criticized what he took to be Kant's overly contemplative and intellectualized conception of aesthetic experience in the *Critique of Judgment*: "Kant was a past-master in first drawing distinctions and then erecting them into compartmental divisions. The effect upon subsequent theory was to give the separation of the esthetic from other modes of experience an alleged scientific basis in the constitution of human nature" (1934, LW 10:257). On the connection between Kant's theory and those of critics such as Fry and Bell, see Nehamas, *Only a Promise of Happiness*.

36. Bell, *Art*, 25.

37. In a striking passage, Dewey writes: "Every intense experience of friendship completes itself artistically" (1934, LW 10:275). And recall the passage that talks about "the delight of the housewife in tending her plants" (1934, LW 10:11).

38. Dewey continues: "There are acts of all kinds that directly refresh and enlarge the spirit and that are instrumental to the production of new

objects and dispositions which are in turn productive of further refine-
ments and replenishments . . . esthetic appreciation is called a good in
itself, or that strange thing an end in itself. But . . . in being preemi-
nently fructifying the things designated means are immediate satis-
factions. They are their own excuses for being just because they are
charged with an office in quickening apprehension, enlarging the hori-
zon of vision" (1925, LW 1:274).

The idea that creative acts of this sort "are their own excuses for
being" because of their lifelong enriching quality breaks down the rigid
separation between instrumental and consummatory aspects. It also
lends further support to my earlier suggestion that Dewey would have
probably explained the "exaltation" offered to us by fine art not in terms
of "super-human" ecstasy (defended by critics such as Bell), but as
something that accompanies this sort of enrichment. He would have
probably said that they *feel* "super-human" to us because they help us
refashion ourselves and our experience.

39. In recent years, philosophers have made important contributions to the
conversation. See, for example, Catherine Z. Elgin, "Art and Educa-
tion," in *The Oxford Handbook of Philosophy of Education*, ed. Harvey
Siegel (Oxford University Press, 2009), 319–32; Kitcher, *The Main
Enterprise of the World*; Moody-Adams, "Philosophy and the Art of
Human Flourishing"; Nehamas, *Only a Promise of Happiness*; Martha
Nussbaum, *Not for Profit: Why Democracy Needs the Humanities* (Princ-
eton, NJ: Princeton University Press, 2010).

40. For the view Dewey was rejecting, see H. L. Mencken's "Shall We
Abolish School Frills? Yes," collected alongside Dewey's response in
(1933, LW 9:406–11).

41. Note that Dewey also argued in favor of making the students' engagement with other subjects more creative and engaging. On this point,
see "Appreciation and Cultivation," where Dewey writes: "What then
is appreciation? What is its nature that it may extend to all subjects
and themes? Literature and the fine arts may give us the key to the
answer. For while not having a monopoly of power to arouse appreciation, they exemplify it in a conspicuous way" (1931, LW 6:113). "Appreciation and Cultivation" argues in favor of creative, active engagement
with all subjects, not just the arts: "Think over the teachers that you
would call inspiring and you will find that they were the teachers who

made you aware of possibilities in the things which they taught and who bred in you desire to realize those possibilities for yourself" (1931, LW 6:117). The essay complements Dewey's project in *Art as Experience*. It highlights the importance of the self's involvement with the material at hand, the transformation that occurs in the process of appreciation, and the importance of treating subjects as still open, to be developed by students. (This resonates with passages in *Art as Experience* where Dewey argues in favor of *developing* aesthetic objects, and not just relying on existing schemes).

42. Dewey wasn't alone in this. See also W. E. B. Du Bois's eloquent defense of the humanities and the arts (especially in the context of racial oppression) in, for instance, *The Education of Black People: Ten Critiques* (New York: Monthly Review Press, 2001), 150. On Du Bois's *Souls*, see Robert Gooding-Williams, *In the Shadow of Du Bois: Afromodern Political Thought in America* (Cambridge, MA: Harvard University Press, 2009). On Du Bois's aesthetics, see Robert Gooding-Williams, "Beauty as Propaganda: On the Political Aesthetics of W. E. B. Du Bois," *Philosophical Topics* 49, no. 1 (2021): 13–34. On the affinities between Du Bois and Dewey, see Paul C. Taylor, *Black Is Beautiful: A Philosophy of Black Aesthetics* (New York: Wiley, 2016), 92.

43. Of course, other arts are also important. For instance, see Moody-Adams, "Philosophy and the Art of Human Flourishing" for an analysis of the educative power of architecture, film, photography, and music.

44. There are some interesting resonances here with Du Bois's aesthetics. I am indebted to Robert Gooding-Williams for pointing this out to me. On the political aspects of Du Bois's aesthetics, see Gooding-Williams, "Beauty as Propaganda," 13–34.

45. Ellen Winner, *How Art Works: A Psychological Exploration* (New York: Oxford University Press, 2019), 189–210. I am indebted to Philip Kitcher for bringing this to my attention.

46. Rilke, *The Poetry of Rilke*, 108–9, my emphasis.

47. Rainer Maria Rilke, *Rilke's Book of Hours: Love Poems to God*, trans. Anita Barrows and Joanna Macy (New York: Riverhead Books, 2005), 223, 233, 219.

48. See, for instance, "Pont du Carrousel," a poem about a blind man (presumably seen by Rilke in Paris on the eponymous bridge over the

Seine). Rilke, *The Poetry of Rilke*, 70–71. *Childhood* allows us to inhabit the perspective of a shy, sensitive, lonely child. We learn to see the strangeness of the grown-up world through the boy's eyes. Rilke, *The Poetry of Rilke*, 56–59.

49. Rilke, *Rilke's Book of Hours*, 217.

50. See, for instance, the critique of city life in Rilke, *Rilke's Book of Hours*, 195–97.

51. Rilke, *Rilke's Book of Hours*, 217.

52. W. E. B. Du Bois, *The Souls of Black Folk*, ed. David W. Blight and Robert Gooding-Williams (New York: Bedford/St. Martin's, 1997), 41–42.

53. I am indebted to Robert-Gooding Williams for steering me in the direction of Du Bois's "Of Beauty and Death" and for illuminating conversations on the subject, from which I have learned much. W. E. B. Du Bois, *Darkwater: Voices from Within the Veil* (New York: Dover Publications, 1999), 130–44.

54. Du Bois, *Darkwater*, ix.

55. For an analysis of Du Bois's notion of sympathy (and of the way it is reflected in *Souls*), see Gooding-Williams, *In the Shadow of Du Bois*. Gooding-Williams also provides an in-depth analysis of how Du Bois achieves this in *Jesus Christ in Texas*. See Gooding-Williams, "Beauty as Propaganda."

56. For a contemporary account of how the arts can help promote reconciliation across social divisions, see Michele M. Moody-Adams, "Civic Art of Remembrance and the Democratic Imagination," 56th Annual Bishop Hurst Lecture, American University, 2015, and "Philosophy and the Art of Human Flourishing."

57. The title of this section is taken from Toni Morrison's Nobel Lecture, https://www.nobelprize.org/prizes/literature/1993/morrison/lecture/, which is extensively quoted herein.

58. For a contemporary answer to this question that resonates with Dewey's view, see also Moody-Adams, "Civic Art of Remembrance and the Democratic Imagination" and "Philosophy and the Art of Human Flourishing." Moody-Adams argues that art can promote social harmony (in a noncoercive manner) by helping us recognize our shared humanity. It can also become a form of protest against injustice.

59. Dewey's view on this seems to resonate with recent philosophical discussions. See Philip S. Kitcher, *Deaths in Venice* (New York: Columbia University Press, 2013); Moody-Adams, "Philosophy and the Art of Human Flourishing."

60. Note the context in which Dewey offered this quotation from Tolstoy. He was reflecting on the importance of the arts in an age that focuses too much on "means:" "Man's command over the means of life, his industrial conquest, seems only to have sharpened prior existing social inequities, to have led to the devotion to the *means* of life at the expense of its serious and significant ends—a noble, free and happy life in which all men participate on something like equal terms" (*Unpublished Writings*, ca. 1910–11, LW 17:391). The arts help us explore what "a noble, free and happy life" might look like. In doing this, they contribute to the larger project of human development outlined in chapter 1.

61. Kitcher also suggests that the arts can help us "appreciate new possibilities," that they can help us conduct "experiments in imagination" (*Deaths in Venice*, 15): "the stimulation of the imagination through literature or music might play an essential role in generating a new perspective on what has hitherto been taken for granted" (17).

62. I see my reconstruction of Dewey's view as complementary to Michele M. Moody-Adams's arguments about the importance of the arts to human flourishing and to the vitality of democracy. See Moody-Adams, "Philosophy and the Art of Human Flourishing."

63. For instance, Nehamas seems to think that beauty moves us without ever fully satisfying—when it prompts us to reach beyond ourselves, it offers us "only a promise of happiness." See *Only a Promise of Happiness*. This way of understanding aesthetic experience seems to stand in tension with Dewey's emphasis on "the consummatory."

64. Robert Musil, *Precision and Soul: Essays and Addresses*, ed. B. Pike and D. S. Luft (Chicago: University of Chicago Press, 1990), 244–45.

65. Musil, *Precision and Soul*, 243–45.

66. We can try to make sense of Dewey's remarks about the "unification" of character by connecting them to his reflections on the fragmentation that results when human beings engage in "routine," mechanical, uncreative activities (such as those of the factory worker forced to produce things according to a predetermined pattern). Dewey's concerns

about this resonate with Ralph Waldo Emerson's. See Emerson, "The American Scholar," in *Essays and Lectures*, ed. Joel Porte (New York: Library of America, 1983), 53–71. Many thanks to Philip Kitcher for pointing out this connection.

67. Moody-Adams, "Philosophy and the Art of Human Flourishing."

68. Gooding-Williams, "Beauty as Propaganda"; Moody-Adams, "Civic Art of Remembrance and the Democratic Imagination" and "Philosophy and the Art of Human Flourishing"; Richard Schusterman, *Pragmatist Aesthetics: Living Beauty, Rethinking Art* (Malden, MA: Blackwell, 1992), 201–35.

69. Clement Greenberg, *Art and Culture* (Boston: Beacon Press, 1961), 18–19.

70. See José Ortega y Gasset, *Dehumanization of Art and Other Essays on Art, Culture, and Literature* (Princeton, NJ: Princeton University Press, 1968), 52, 7.

71. For philosophical accounts of the value of the arts that resonate with these concerns, see also Elgin, "Art and Education"; Gooding-Williams, "Beauty as Propaganda"; Kitcher, *The Main Enterprise of the World*; Moody-Adams, "Philosophy and the Art of Human Flourishing"; and Nussbaum, *Not for Profit*, among others. For another critique of these, see also Nehamas, *Only a Promise of Happiness*.

4. FLOURISHING AND EDUCATION

1. For example, a number of contributions to scholarship on Deweyan democracy side-step questions about education in order to focus on issues of epistemic justification. Matthew Festenstein examines whether Dewey had "an epistemic argument for democracy"; see Festenstein, "Does Dewey Have an 'Epistemic Argument' for Democracy?," *Contemporary Pragmatism* 16, no. 2–3 (2019): 217–41. Cheryl Misak focuses on the relationship between democracy and inquiry; see Misak, *The American Pragmatists* (New York: Oxford University Press, 2013), 136. James Bohman focuses on the "epistemic division of labor" in Deweyan democracy; see Bohman, "Participation Through Publics: Did Dewey Answer Lippmann?," *Contemporary Pragmatism* 7, no. 1 (2010): 49–68. Melvin Rogers focuses on issues of expertise; see Rogers, "Dewey, Pluralism, and Democracy: A Response to Robert

Talisse," *Transactions of the Charles S. Peirce Society* 45, no. 1 (2009): 69–91. The focus of this book is different. It adds to the existing literature by arguing for the centrality of education to Dewey's philosophical project (including his thought on democracy).

2. See the account of the educative value of everyday interactions in a democracy in "Creative Democracy—The Task Before Us" (1939, LW 14:224–30). See also the critique of the remoteness of museum art, particularly as conceptualized by certain art critics, from the lived experience of individuals and communities in *Art as Experience* (1934, LW 10:12–15).

3. W. E. B. Du Bois saw the education of children as "the problem of problems." Du Bois, *Darkwater: Voices from Within the Veil* (New York: Dover Publications, 1999), 114. Plato devoted a surprising amount of attention to the way in which the arts educate the young (see Plato, *Republic*, Book III). Jean-Jacques Rousseau went as far as taking the practice of putting babies in swaddling-clothes as a philosophical issue; Rousseau, *Emile*, trans. Alan Bloom (New York: Basic Books, 1979), 43.

4. As I have tried to show in this book, this question was of particular interest to Du Bois and to Dewey. Du Bois reflected on how education might further social progress by preparing African Americans to take part in bringing it about. On this issue, see, for example, Du Bois, *The Souls of Black Folk*, ed. David W. Blight and Robert Gooding-Williams (New York: Bedford/St. Martin's, 1997), 172–84. Dewey took seriously the question of how we might educate human beings so that they would, in turn, help improve these arrangements by their own efforts, through the way they live and relate to others. This is at the heart of his conception of the democratic character.

5. William James, "The Sentiment of Rationality," in *William James: Writings 1878–1899*, ed. John J. McDermott (New York: Library of America, 1992).

6. In *Democracy and Education*, Dewey acknowledges Plato's influence: "Much which has been said so far is borrowed from what Plato first consciously taught the world" (1916; MW 9: 94). For some other interesting expressions of Dewey's admiration for Plato, see "The Ethics of Democracy" (1888, EW 1:241) and "The 'Socratic Dialogues' of Plato" (1925, LW 2:140).

7. For an illuminating analysis of the ethical and political significance of subjects that seem apparently irrelevant to ruling the city (such as geometry and mathematics) in Plato's ideal curriculum, see Myles F. Burnyeat, "Plato on Why Mathematics Is Good for the Soul," *Proceedings of the British Academy* 103 (2000): 1–81.

8. For an analysis of the centrality of educational concerns to Plato's critique of the arts, see Myles F. Burnyeat, "Culture and Society in Plato's Republic," Tanner Lectures on Human Values, delivered at Harvard University on December 10–12, 1997, https://tannerlectures .org/lectures/culture-and-society-in-platos-republic/

9. Some worry that Dewey's notion of growth is too prescriptive—this is the worry at the heart of Talisse's contention that Deweyan democracy is incompatible with pluralism (Talisse, "A Farewell to Deweyan Democracy," 509–26). Talisse argues that Deweyan democracy is rooted in what he calls, drawing on Rawls, a "comprehensive moral doctrine"— namely, that of growth. However, Talisse does not unpack the Deweyan notion of growth; arguably, this notion is significantly more open-ended than he acknowledges. The notion of growth, when properly understood, serves to empower individuals to take part in deciding how to live (in a conversation with others), instead of forcing them to subscribe to some complete, antecedently formulated doctrine. Of course, even with this in mind, one could still worry that being committed to taking part in the Deweyan democratic conversation—and developing the necessary habits, such as sympathy and open-mindedness—might conflict with the commitments of some individuals and/or groups, and if so, it might still be in tension with "pluralism." Dewey's conception of growth is certainly not completely neutral. But it is more open-ended than he is sometimes given credit for. In this, Dewey may have been inspired by Hegel (although Dewey eventually disavowed his early Hegelianism in favor of a perspective informed by Darwinian evolutionary biology). On the connection between Dewey and Hegel, see Richard Bernstein, *The Pragmatic Turn* (London: Polity, 2010), 91–92; Stephen Rockefeller, *John Dewey: Religious Faith and Democratic Humanism* (New York: Columbia University Press, 1991), 236–37.

10. For a contemporary exploration of these issues, see Philip S. Kitcher, *The Main Enterprise of the World: Rethinking Education* (New York: Oxford University Press, 2021).

11. On this issue, see Kitcher, *The Main Enterprise of the World*.

12. See, for example, *Emile*, 33.

13. Rousseau, *Emile*, 40.

14. Whether Rousseau saw himself as having succeeded—and whether he thought this harmony between the "natural" human being and the "citizen" is in principle attainable—is debatable. Rousseau writes: "I will be told that I, too, dream. I agree; but I give my dreams *as dreams*, which others are not careful to do, leaving it to the reader to find out *whether they contain something useful for people who are awake*" (Rousseau, *Emile*, 112, my emphases).

15. For an in-depth analysis of Rousseau's understanding of these dynamics, see Frederick Neuhouser, *Rousseau's Theodicy of Self-Love: Evil, Rationality, and the Drive for Recognition* (New York: Oxford University Press, 2008).

16. Rousseau, *Emile*, 38. This, of course, couldn't be further from Dewey's conception of the proper education of the child, which focuses on the child's communicative and cooperative skills in diverse communities and exposure to a wide range of perspectives. But the idea that the reigning social arrangements are bad and that education should be to some extent removed from them was not completely alien to Dewey—there are some passages in which he criticizes the prejudices and customs of the wider society and suggests that in schools we should strive to create "idealized communities" (communities that are, among other things, cooperative and inclusive); those "idealized communities" would then educate citizens who would change the wider social arrangements for the better. In *Democracy and Education*, Dewey writes that in schools "we may produce a projection in type of the society we should like to realize, and by forming minds in accord with it gradually modify the larger and more recalcitrant features of adult society" (1916, MW 9:326). The Deweyan democratic character is educated precisely to take part in progressive social change.

17. Plato, *Republic*, 169.

18. Dewey seems to have formulated his views independently of reading Marx (since *Democracy and Education* was published in 1916 and Marx's *Economic and Philosophical Manuscripts of 1844* was not available until 1932). I thank Philip Kitcher for pointing this out to me.

19. Some scholars have tried to rescue Rousseau by suggesting that his views on the education of Sophie are irrelevant to the main line of his argument, which can be separated from them. See, e.g., Neuhouser, *Rousseau's Theodicy of Self-Love.* I do not think so—on my view, Rousseau anchors the ethical education of Emile in his relationship with Sophie. In Rousseau's scheme, Sophie is to be "the angel in the house" (as Woolf might have put it), in order to be the anchor for Emile's romantic (and "chivalric") conception of virtue. The gender bias of *Emile* raises worries about some of the pitfalls described here.

20. Rousseau, *Emile*, 361, 359.

21. Du Bois, *Darkwater*, 114, my emphases.

22. Du Bois, *Darkwater*, 117, 121.

23. Du Bois's *Education of Black People*, which contains his addresses to African American colleges, is also full of sharp criticism of educational programs designed with narrowly conceived vocational training as a goal. See Du Bois, *The Education of Black People: Ten Critiques* (New York: Monthly Review Press, 2001). In a passage that seems to resonate in striking ways with Dewey's concerns, Du Bois conceives of "the main end of democracy . . . [as] not only that the complaints of all should be heard, or the hurts of the humblest healed; *it is for the vastly larger object of loosing the possibilities of mankind* for the development of a higher and broader and more varied human culture." Du Bois, *Darkwater*, 154, my emphasis.

24. See Du Bois, *The Education of Black People*, 65–66. Genuine life, for Du Bois, involves the freedom of spirit experienced in such aesthetic moments, when one rises above "the little sordid things of the earth." On this point, see also the analysis in Robert Gooding-Williams, *In the Shadow of Du Bois: Afro-modern Political Thought in America* (Cambridge, MA: Harvard University Press, 2009).

25. Du Bois, *The Education of Black People*, 150, my emphasis.

26. Du Bois, *The Education of Black People*, 151.

27. On this issue, see Gooding-Williams, *In the Shadow of Du Bois.*

28. On the affinities between Du Bois and Dewey, see Paul C. Taylor, *Black Is Beautiful: A Philosophy of Black Aesthetics* (New York: Wiley, 2016), 92. There Taylor argues that Du Bois should be read as an "expressivist" who had affinities with Marx and Dewey: "But the most

useful examples for studying Du Bois are Marx and Dewey. Both the Marxian and Deweyan revisions of Hegel's narrative insist on holistic self-cultivation and, in good romantic fashion, reject the alienation of modern industrial civilization. On both approaches, ethical life is bound up with an essentially artistic or poetic revisioning of the landscape of agentive possibility, and human personalities are always works in progress, fashioned at the intersection of community resources, social conditions, and ethical agency. In addition, both see individual human subjects as expressions of deeper cultural and material forces."

29. Du Bois, *Darkwater*, 59.

30. Dewey's formulation that education can be a "systematic means" to the "good life" may obscure an important Deweyan view that a life of flourishing is just a life of constant growth (understood as a lifelong revision of habits). If education is understood specifically as such personal growth, then it can be seen as central to a flourishing life (and not just as a means to an end). There seems to be some affinity between Du Bois's view on this and Dewey's. Du Bois and Dewey seem to have both held a conception of education as a life-long process of enrichment. Du Bois's discussion of a "life that is more than meat" (*The Education of Black People*, 150) centers on what seems like a potentially lifelong development of human capacities.

31. Du Bois, *Darkwater*, 59.

BIBLIOGRAPHY

§1. WORKS BY DEWEY

Abbreviations

EW   John Dewey, *The Early Works: 1882–1898*, 5 volumes, edited by Jo Ann Boydston. Carbondale: Southern Illinois University Press, 1969–1972.

MW   John Dewey, *The Middle Works: 1899–1924*, 15 volumes, edited by Jo Ann Boydston. Carbondale: Southern Illinois University Press, 1976–1983.

LW   John Dewey, *The Later Works: 1925–1953*, 17 volumes, edited by Jo Ann Boydston. Carbondale: Southern Illinois University Press, 1981–1992.

Dewey Works Cited

"The Ethics of Democracy" (1888). EW 1:227–49.

"A College Course: What Should I Expect From It?" (1890). EW 3:51–55.

"The Aesthetic Element in Education" (1897). EW 5:202–3.

"The Place of Manual Training in the Elementary Course of Study" (1901). MW 1:230–37.

"The School as Social Centre" (1902). MW 2:80–93.

"Democracy in Education" (1903). MW 3:229–39.

"Democracy and Education" (1916). MW 9:1–370.

"The Need for a Recovery of Philosophy" (1917). MW 10:3–48.

"Philosophy and Democracy" (1919). MW 11:41–53.

"Reconstruction in Philosophy" (1920). MW 12:80–201.

"Social Absolutism" (1921). MW 13:311–16.

"Racial Prejudice and Friction" (1922). MW 13:242–54.

"Mediocrity and Individuality" (1922). MW 13:289–94.

"Individuality, Equality and Superiority" (1922). MW 13:295–300.

"Education as Politics" (1922). MW 13:329–34.

"Review of Public Opinion by Walter Lippmann" (1922).
    MW 13:337–44.

"Human Nature and Conduct" (1922). MW 14:1–227.

"Experience and Nature" (1925). LW 1:1–326.

"The 'Socratic Dialogues' of Plato" (1925). LW 2:124–40.

"Practical Democracy: Review of Lippmann's The Phantom Public" (1925).
    LW 2:213–20.

"The Public and Its Problems" (1927). LW 2:235–372.

"The Quest for Certainty" (1929). LW 4:1–250.

"From Absolutism to Experimentalism" (1930). LW 5:147–60.

"Individualism, Old and New" (1930). LW 5:41–123.

"Philosophy and Education" (1930). LW 5:289–98.

"Appreciation and Cultivation" (1931). LW 6:112–17.

"Shall We Abolish School 'Frills?' " (1933). LW 9:141–46.

"Why Have Progressive Schools?" (1933). LW 9:147–57.

"Education for a Changing Social Order" (1934). LW 9:158–68.

"Education and the Social Order" (1934). LW 9:175–85.

"Character Training for Youth" (1934). LW 9:186–93.

"The Need for a Philosophy of Education" (1934). LW 9:194–204.

"Art as Experience" (1934). LW 10:1–352.

"Liberalism and Social Action" (1935). LW 11:1–65.

"The Challenge of Democracy to Education" (1937). LW 11:181–90.

"Democracy Is Radical" (1937). LW 11:296–99.

"Logic: The Theory of Inquiry" (1938). LW 12:1–528.

"Experience and Education" (1938). LW 13:1–62.

"I Believe" (1939). LW 14:91–97.

"Creative Democracy—The Task Before Us" (1939). LW 14:224–30.

"Art as Our Heritage" (1940). LW 14:255–57.

"Contrary to Human Nature" (1940). LW 14:258–61.

"The Meaning of the Term: Liberalism" (1940). LW 14:252–54.

"Address of Welcome to the League for Industrial Democracy" (1941). LW 14:262–65.

"Lessons from the War—In Philosophy" (1941). LW 14:312–34.

"The Basic Values and Loyalties of Democracy" (1941). LW 14:275–77

"For a New Education" (1941). LW 14:278–80.

"What Is Democracy?" (1946). LW 14:471–74.

"Aesthetic Experience as a Primary Phase and as Artistic Development" (1950). LW 16:395–98.

"John Dewey Responds" (1950). LW 17:84–87.

"Education for a New and Better World" (Unpublished). LW 17:475–79.

"Tolstoi's Art" (Unpublished). LW 17:381–92.

§2. WORKS BY OTHER AUTHORS

Anderson, Elizabeth. "Fair Opportunity in Education: A Democratic Equality Perspective." *Ethics* 117, no. 4 (2007): 595–622.

Bakhurst, David. *The Formation of Reason*. New York: Wiley-Blackwell, 2011.

Bell, Clive. *Art*. New York: Capricorn Books, 1958.

Bernstein, Richard. "Creative Democracy—The Task Still Before Us." *American Journal of Theology and Philosophy* 21, no. 3 (2000): 215–28.

——. *The Pragmatic Turn*. London: Polity, 2010.

Bohman, James. "Participation Through Publics: Did Dewey Answer Lippmann?" *Contemporary Pragmatism* 7, no. 1 (2010): 49–68.

Brighouse, Harry. *On Education*. New York: Routledge, 2006.

Burnyeat, Myles F. "Culture and Society in Plato's Republic." Tanner Lectures on Human Values, delivered at Harvard University on December 10–12, 1997. https://tannerlectures.org/lectures/culture-and-society-in-platos-republic/.

——. "Plato on Why Mathematics Is Good for the Soul." *Proceedings of the British Academy* 103 (2000): 1–81.

Cooper, John M. *Six Ways of Life in Ancient Philosophy from Socrates to Plotinus*. Princeton, NJ: Princeton University Press, 2012.

Curren, Randall. "Justice, Instruction, and the Good: The Case for Public Education in Aristotle and Plato's Laws, Part I—Groundwork for an Interpretation of Politics VIII.1." *Studies in Philosophy and Education* 11, no. 4 (1993): 293–311.

——. "Justice, Instruction, and the Good: The Case for Public Education in Aristotle and Plato's Laws, Part II—Why Education Is Important Enough to Merit the Legislator's Attention." *Studies in Philosophy and Education* 12, nos. 2–4 (1993): 103–26.

——. "Justice, Instruction, and the Good: The Case for Public Education in Aristotle and Plato's Laws, Part III—Why Education Should Be Public and the Same for All." *Studies in Philosophy and Education* 13, no. 1 (1994): 1–31.

——. "Pragmatist Philosophy of Education." In *The Oxford Handbook of Philosophy of Education*, edited by Harvey Siegel, 489–507. New York: Oxford University Press, 2009.

Curren, Randall, and Charles Dorn. *Patriotic Education in a Global Age.* Chicago: University of Chicago Press, 2018.

Du Bois, W. E. B. *Darkwater: Voices from Within the Veil.* New York: Dover Publications, 1999.

——. *The Education of Black People: Ten Critiques.* New York: Monthly Review Press, 2001.

——. *The Souls of Black Folk.* Edited by David W. Blight and Robert Gooding-Williams. New York: Bedford/St. Martin's, 1997.

Elgin, Catherine Z. "Art and Education." In *The Oxford Handbook of Philosophy of Education*, edited by Harvey Siegel, 319–32. New York: Oxford University Press, 2009.

——. "Education and the Advancement of Understanding." In *Philosophy of Education*, edited by Randall Curren, 417–22. Malden, MA: Blackwell, 2007.

Emerson, Ralph W. "The American Scholar." In *Essays and Lectures*, 53–71. New York: Library of America, 1983.

Fesmire, Steven. "Democracy and the Industrial Imagination in American Education." *Education and Culture* 32, no. 1 (2016): 53–61.

——. *Dewey.* New York: Routledge, 2015.

Festenstein, Matthew. "Does Dewey Have an 'Epistemic Argument' for Democracy?" *Contemporary Pragmatism* 16, no. 2–3 (2019): 217–41.

——. "The Ties of Communication: Dewey on Ideal and Political Democracy." *History of Political Thought* 18, no. 1 (1997): 104–24.

Fry, Roger. *Vision and Design.* Oxford: Oxford University Press, 1981.

Gooding-Williams, Robert. "Beauty as Propaganda: On the Political Aesthetics of W. E. B. Du Bois." *Philosophical Topics* 49, no. 1 (2021): 13–34.

——. *In the Shadow of Du Bois: Afro-modern Political Thought in America.* Cambridge, MA: Harvard University Press, 2009.

——. "Pessimism and Beauty in Du Bois' Darkwater." Unpublished manuscript.

Greenberg, Clement. *Art and Culture.* Boston: Beacon Press, 1961.

Gutmann, Amy. *Democratic Education.* Princeton, NJ: Princeton University Press, 1999.

Hegel, Georg W. F. *Elements of the Philosophy of Right.* Edited by Allen W. Wood, translated by H. B. Nisbet. Cambridge: Cambridge University Press, 1991.

Honneth, Axel. "Education and the Democratic Public Sphere: A Neglected Chapter of Political Philosophy." In *Recognition and Freedom: Axel Honneth's Political Thought*, edited by J. Jakobsen and O. Lysaker, 17–32. Leiden: Brill, 2015.

——. *The I in We: Studies in the Theory of Recognition.* London: Polity Press, 2012.

Jackson, Jeff. *Equality Beyond Debate: John Dewey's Pragmatic Idea of Democracy.* New York: Cambridge University Press, 2018.

Jaeggi, Rahel. *Alienation.* New York: Columbia University Press, 2014.

James, William. *Principles of Psychology.* Cambridge, MA: Harvard University Press, 1983.

——. "The Sentiment of Rationality." In *William James: Writings 1878–1899.* New York: Library of America, 1992.

Kitcher, Philip S. *Deaths in Venice.* New York: Columbia University Press, 2013.

——. "Dewey's Conception of Philosophy." In *The Oxford Handbook of Dewey*, edited by Steven Fesmire, 3–22. New York: Oxford University Press, 2017.

——. *The Main Enterprise of the World: Rethinking Education.* New York: Oxford University Press, 2021.

——. *Moral Progress.* New York: Oxford University Press, 2021.

——. *Preludes to Pragmatism: Toward a Reconstruction of Philosophy.* New York: Oxford University Press, 2012.

——. "Social Progress." *Social Philosophy and Policy* 34, no. 2 (2017): 46–65.

Kronman, Anthony. *Education's End: Why Our Colleges and Universities Have Given up on the Meaning of Life.* New Haven, CT: Yale University Press, 2007.

Levinson, Meira. *The Demands of Liberal Education*. New York: Oxford University Press, 1999.

——. *No Citizen Left Behind*. Cambridge, MA: Harvard University Press, 2012.

Lippmann, Walter. *The Phantom Public*. New Brunswick, NJ: Transaction Publishers, 1993.

——. *Public Opinion*. New York: Free Press, 1997.

Long, A. A., and D. N. Sedley. *The Hellenistic Philosophers*. Cambridge: Cambridge University Press, 2015.

Marx, Karl. *Economic and Philosophic Manuscripts of 1844*. Buffalo, NY: Prometheus Books, 1988.

Misak, Cheryl. *The American Pragmatists*. New York: Oxford University Press, 2013.

Monet, Claude. *Monet by Himself*. Edited by Richard Kendall. New York: Bulfinch Press/Little, Brown and Company, 1989.

Moody-Adams, Michele M. "Civic Art of Remembrance and the Democratic Imagination." 56th Annual Bishop Hurst Lecture, American University, 2015.

——. "Philosophy and the Art of Human Flourishing." In *Philosophy and Flourishing*, edited by James Stuhr and Joseph Pawelski, 214–30. New York: Oxford University Press, 2020.

Morrison, Toni. "Nobel Lecture." https://www.nobelprize.org/prizes /literature/1993/morrison/lecture/

Musil, Robert. *Precision and Soul: Essays and Addresses*. Edited and translated by B. Pike and D. S. Luft. Chicago: University of Chicago Press, 1990.

Nehamas, Alexander. *The Art of Living: Socratic Reflections from Plato to Foucault*. Berkeley: University of California Press, 1998.

——. *Only a Promise of Happiness: The Place of Beauty in a World of Art*. Princeton, NJ: Princeton University Press, 2007.

Neuhouser, Frederick. *Foundations of Hegel's Social Theory: Actualizing Freedom*. Cambridge, MA: Harvard University Press, 2000.

——. *Rousseau's Theodicy of Self-Love: Evil, Rationality, and the Drive for Recognition*. New York: Oxford University Press, 2008.

Nietzsche, Friedrich. *Basic Writings of Nietzsche*. Translated by Walter Kaufmann. New York: Modern Library, 2000.

———. *Untimely Meditations*. Edited by Daniel Breazeale, translated by R. J. Hollingdale. New York: Cambridge University Press, 1997.

Nussbaum, Martha. *Not for Profit: Why Democracy Needs the Humanities*. Princeton, NJ: Princeton University Press, 2010.

Ortega y Gasset, José. *Dehumanization of Art and Other Essays on Art, Culture, and Literature*. Princeton, NJ: Princeton University Press, 1968.

Pappas, Gregory F. *John Dewey's Ethics: Democracy as Experience*. Bloomington: Indiana University Press, 2008.

Peirce, Charles S. "The Fixation of Belief." *Popular Science Monthly* 12 (1877): 1–15.

Peters, Richard S. "Education as Initiation." In *Philosophy of Education: An Anthology*, edited by Randall Curren, 1–4. Malden, MA: Blackwell, 2007.

Plato. *Complete Works*. Edited by John M. Cooper. Indianapolis: Hackett, 1997.

———. *Republic*. Translated by G. M. A. Grube and C. D. C. Reeve. Indianapolis: Hackett, 1992.

Proust, Marcel. *Days of Reading*. Translated by James Sturrock. New York: Penguin Books, 2008.

Rilke, Rainer Maria. *The Poetry of Rilke*. Translated by Edward Snow. Berkeley, CA: North Point Press, 2009.

———. *Rilke's Book of Hours: Love Poems to God*. Translated by Anita Barrows and Joanna Macy. New York: Riverhead Books, 2005.

Rockefeller, Stephen. *John Dewey: Religious Faith and Democratic Humanism*. New York: Columbia University Press, 1991.

Rogers, Melvin L. "Dewey and His Vision of Democracy." *Contemporary Pragmatism* 7, no. 1 (2010): 69–91.

———. "Dewey, Pluralism, and Democracy: A Response to Robert Talisse." *Transactions of the Charles S. Peirce Society* 45, no. 1 (2009): 75–79.

———. "Revisiting *The Public and Its Problems*." In John Dewey, *The Public and Its Problems*, edited by Melvin Rogers, 1–43. Athens, OH: Swallow Press, 2016.

Rorty, Richard. *Achieving Our Country*. Cambridge, MA: Harvard University Press, 1998.

Rousseau, Jean-Jacques. "Discourse on the Origin of Inequality." In *Basic Political Writings*, translated and edited by David A. Cress, 29–120. Indianapolis: Hackett, 1987.

——. *Emile.* Translated by Alan Bloom. New York: Basic Books, 1979.

——. *The Reveries of the Solitary Walker.* Translated by Charles E. Butterworth. Indianapolis: Hackett, 1992.

Ryan, Alan. *John Dewey and the High Tide of American Liberalism.* New York: W. W. Norton, 1995.

Seigfried, Charlene H. "Socializing Democracy: Jane Addams and John Dewey." *Philosophy of the Social Sciences* 29, no. 2 (1999): 207–30.

Shusterman, Richard. *Pragmatist Aesthetics: Living Beauty, Rethinking Art.* Malden, MA: Blackwell, 1992.

Siegel, Harvey. "Introduction: Philosophy of Education and Philosophy." In *The Oxford Handbook of Philosophy of Education*, edited by Harvey Siegel, 3–10. New York: Oxford University Press, 2009.

Spate, Virginia. *Claude Monet: The Color of Time.* London: Thames and Hudson, 1992.

Talisse, Robert B. "A Farewell to Deweyan Democracy." *Political Studies* 59 (2011): 509–26.

Taylor, Paul C. *Black Is Beautiful: A Philosophy of Black Aesthetics.* New York: Wiley, 2016.

Westbrook, Robert. *John Dewey and American Democracy.* Ithaca, NY: Cornell University Press, 1991.

Whitman, Walt. *Democratic Vistas: The Original Edition in Facsimile.* Edited by Ed Folsom. Iowa City: University of Iowa Press, 2010.

Winner, Ellen. *How Art Works: A Psychological Exploration.* New York: Oxford University Press, 2019.

Woolf, Virginia. *A Room of One's Own.* New York: Harcourt, 2005.

Wordsworth, William. *Selected Poems and Prefaces.* Edited by Jack Stillinger. Boston: Houghton Mifflin, 1965.

INDEX

·

GPSR Authorized Representative: Easy Access System Europe, Mustamäe tee 50, 10621 Tallinn, Estonia, gpsr.requests@easproject.com